D1485745

A GOOD·BOOK
IS THE
PRECIOUS
LIFE-BLOOD
OF A
MASTER
SPIRIT
Milton

The KING'S TREASURIES

OF LITERATURE

GENERAL EDITOR

SIR A·T· QUILLER COUCH

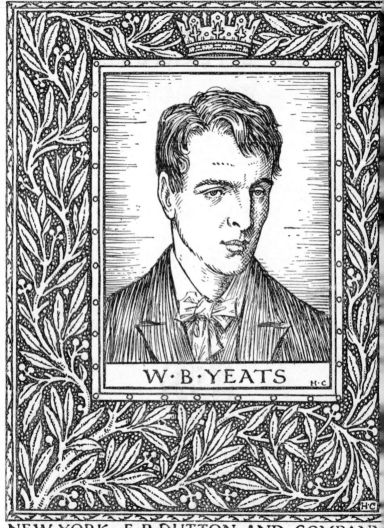

W·B·YEATS

NEW YORK E·P·DUTTON AND COMPANY

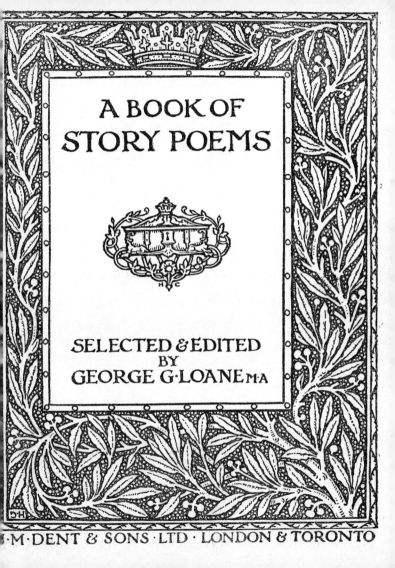

A BOOK OF STORY POEMS

SELECTED & EDITED
BY
GEORGE G·LOANE M·A

·M·DENT & SONS·LTD·LONDON & TORONTO

SOLE AGENT FOR SCOTLAND
THE GRANT EDUCATIONAL CO. LTD.
GLASGOW

FIRST PUBLISHED, 1921.   REPRINTED, 1922, 1923, 1924

PRINTED IN GREAT BRITAIN

CONTENTS

5

6 CONTENTS

ACKNOWLEDGMENTS

For permission to use copyright poems thanks are due and are hereby tendered: to Mr. John Murray for Browning's *Hervé Riel*; to Messrs. T. Fisher Unwin, Ltd., and to Mr. W. B. Yeats for *The Death of Cuchulain* from *Poems: New Edition*; to H. S. H. Guinness, Esq., for Sir Samuel Ferguson's *The Healing of Conall Carnach*; and to Sir H. Newbolt and Mr. John Murray for *Hawke* from *Poems New and Old*.

INTRODUCTION

IT is true of all language that the thing said is not really separable from the way of saying it. If it were differently said, it would be—no matter how slightly— a different thing. "Thanks!" "Thank you!" and "I thank you" differ considerably. The best good story will fail to touch our emotions if it is badly told. And a good story in prose is not so touching as a fine poem on the same subject. The best prose narrative of Sir John Moore's burial cannot compare with Wolfe's lines (XV.); the steady rhythm as of a funeral march is inseparable from the narrative; the whole scene is concentrated and made vivid in a way impossible to prose. Even a less obviously touching story may be transfigured by the poet's imagination and art. Read a prose account of Alpheus and Arethusa, and then read Shelley's poem (XXVI.); the swift rush of the anapæsts, and the cunning choice of beautiful words, grip us immediately; the mere sound excites us; our attention is aroused, and we delight in a new experience. For a poet is a person with stronger and nobler feelings than ours, who can, if we give him the chance, strengthen and ennoble such feelings as we have, and so increase our power. It is not, of course to be expected that everyone will enjoy all (even good) poetry, and if we don't enjoy it, honesty should make us ashamed of pretending to. But the taste for poetry may be cultivated, like other tastes, and it is a possession worth having. And as stories appeal to everyone, this collection ought to be of some use.

Why should a poet have the power of telling stories— and other things—better than prose writers? Partly because he is of necessity an artist in words. Even such straightforward verses as *How they Brought the Good News from Ghent to Aix* must have taken more thought and selection than a simple prose narrative. A poet is bound to write carefully, if only because slovenly poetry is unreadable; while we are unfortunately quite accustomed to slovenly prose. But the poet's chief advantage lies in the fact mentioned— that the metre rouses our attention and so increases our power of perception. The cunning fellow knows that, and presumes on it. He economises his words, and so increases their effect. There is a good example in No. XXXIV.

> His teeth were strong, the cage was wood—
> He left poor Bully's beak.

Notice how much is omitted in *The Death of Cuchulain*, and how the quality of its pathos is affected thereby. Then the mere pleasure of rhythmical sound is an advantage, for we are thereby put into the right mood unawares. Sound is of the essence of poetry. As a maxim for poets, the advice " take care of the sound and the sense will take care of itself " may be liable to abuse; but for the readers of poetry—and all poetry should be read aloud, until our inward ear is acute—the advice is a command. The effects of metre are many. It may be stirring and harp-like as in *Agincourt*, or stirring and hammer-like as in *Naseby*; it may dance with elfin tread as in *The Lady of Shalott*, move swiftly and lightly as in *The Sensitive Plant*, gallop as in *Lochinvar*, or pace solemnly as in *Laodamia* and *Hohenlinden*; or it may do all these things, and others, as in *Alexander's Feast*.

This collection illustrates some of the many ways of telling a story in verse. The Story Poem *par excellence* would be the epic, a long poem describing some great action, with a " hero " of course, and with all its parts so closely wrought into the main theme that none could be removed without loss to the whole. Such poems are naturally rare; the *Iliad* and *Odyssey* of Homer, and Milton's *Paradise Lost*, occur most readily to the mind. Again, every drama in verse is a Story Poem; but these also are too big for us. However, in many of our poems the dramatic element is important. This is especially true of our only example of the old ballads, *Sir Patrick Spens*, and it occurs in their modern imitations, *e.g. Lord Ullin's Daughter*, *Alice Brand*, and *Rosabelle*; in all these the characters tell part of the story. This is natural; for the ballad had its origin in a sort of village *ballet* or story in action, where the chief characters might sing or say their words, and the general company contribute the refrain. Story poems without the length, seriousness, or artistic unity of the epic, are called narrative or lyrical according as the historical or the emotional element is the more prominent. Chaucer was a great narrative poet, and so was his disciple Morris; *The Life and Death of Jason*, of which

No. XX. is a small portion, is not an epic, because the adventures described are not a part of one great action. A biography might indeed make an epic, but only if the whole life recorded was spent in carrying out some one idea. Spenser's *Faerie Queene* was meant to be an epic, but was never completed. When the story is merely a vehicle for satire, as in Butler's *Hudibras*, the poem is naturally classed among satires; but Pope's delightful *Rape of the Lock* is really a mock-epic. Dryden wrote some admirable narrative poems at the very end of his life. Burns's *Tam o' Shanter* is an excellent example of the lighter sort. Crabbe's tales of provincial life are generally sombre, but powerful and full of observation. When we come to the nineteenth century, the distinction between narrative and lyrical tends to break down. Such poems as Coleridge's *Ancient Mariner* and Keats's *Eve of St. Agnes* are on the border line. Scott and Byron wrote long narrative poems in lyric measures. We are on clearer ground again with Tennyson's *Idylls of the King*, *English Idylls*, and poems like *Enoch Arden*, Matthew Arnold's *Sohrab and Rustum*, Swinburne's *St. Dorothy*, Morris's *Earthly Paradise*, and Ferguson's fine versions of Irish sagas, which are at last winning recognition. In fact, what Chaucer and Dryden did for their generations—the dressing up of old stories in the language and general poetic outfit of later times —was done for the nineteenth century by the writers just mentioned; but Tennyson, especially in his later *Idylls*, modernised or sanctified the characters so much that some people prefer to read the tales in the old

prose of Sir Thomas Malory. Fine examples of ballad
and lyrical Story Poems, for one reason or another
not given here, are Hood's *The Dream of Eugene Aram*,
Rossetti's *Sister Helen*, Buchanan's *Ballad of Judas
Iscariot*, Morris's *The Haystack in the Floods*, Mere-
dith's *The Death of Attila* and *The Young Princess*,
and Kipling's *Ballad of East and West*. An interesting
variety of Story Poem was invented by Edward Lear
in his nonsense poems, such as *The Jumblies*. Here
the sound has asserted itself above the sense, and yet
the sense has a queer sort of coherence which forbids
us to despise it. Perhaps we attempt the impossible
when we try to separate the two. Sir W. S. Gilbert's
Bab Ballads are also admirable in their special way,
a way so special that the recognised adjective " Gil-
bertian " is the only short description. *Captain Reece*
or *The Rival Curates* would have adorned this collection.

The connection of the Story and the Poem may be
of three kinds. The story may be (1) the immediate
cause of the emotion which produces the poem, (2) a
means chosen for expressing some thought or emotion
to which the poet wishes to give form, or (3) a sort
of ground-work for poetic embroidery. *The Burial of
Sir John Moore* is one good example of the first class,
and *An Incident of the French Camp* looks like another.
Just as clearly *The Sensitive Plant*, *The Forsaken
Merman*, and *Lucy Gray* belong to the second class.
Sometimes it is hard to say to which of the two a
poem, *e.g. Arethusa*, should be assigned. Story Poems
of these two classes will in general be lyrics; those of
the third class will in general be narrative poems.

Such in this collection are *Jason's Ploughing, The Healing of Conall Carnach,* and *The Hermit* ; for it does not follow that a poem with a moral was written for the moral's sake. Worthy Dr. Parnell may have imagined that he was vindicating the ways of God to man, but we are at liberty to think that he was enjoying the effective rendering of a good story. *Alexander's Feast*—like Pindar's *Odes*, of which it is an imitation—is a miracle, for it is a fine lyric made to order, expressing emotions deliberately called up, not spontaneous. It seems to belong to both our second and third classes. *Laodamia*, on the other hand, is the expression of an intense personal emotion, yet it is rather long and stiff for a lyric; however, that is a debatable point.

The phrase " poetic embroidery " was used above. It is perhaps a dubious phrase, for it might conceivably suggest that poetic language is a mere decorative addition to plain sense. Let us therefore recur to our opening statement, which shows the futility of that view; and let us notice further that when a poet " embroiders," his materials are not ultimately his words, but the thoughts and emotions expressed by those words; and in all good poetry those thoughts and emotions are such as arise naturally from the subject, whether that is borrowed or invented; they are inseparable parts of the subject as the poet's rich nature conceives it, and in nowise mere ornaments.

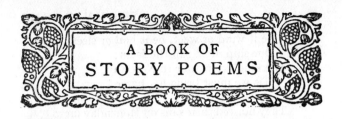

A BOOK OF
STORY POEMS

I. SIR PATRICK SPENS

THE king sits in Dumfermline town,
   Drinking the blude-red wine:
" O whare will I get a skeely skipper
   To sail this new ship o' mine? "

O up and spake an eldern knight
   Sat at the king's right knee:
" Sir Patrick Spens is the best sailor
   That ever sailed the sea."

Our king has written a braid letter
   And sealed it wi' his hand,   **10**
And sent it to Sir Patrick Spens,
   Was walking on the sands.

" To Noroway, to Noroway,
   To Noroway o'er the faem;
The king's daughter to Noroway,
   'Tis thou maun bring her hame."

3. *Skeely*. Skilly, skilful.
9. *Braid*. Broad, open; not a closed roll.
14. *Faem*. Foam.   16. *Maun*. Must.

" Be it wind or weet, be it hail or sleet,
   Our ship must sail the faem;
The king's daughter to Noroway,
   'Tis we must bring her hame."   20

They hoisted their sails on Monenday morn
   Wi' a' the speed they may;
They hae landed safe in Noroway
   Upon a Wodensday.

They hadna been a week, a week,
   In Noroway but twae,
When that the lords o' Noroway
   Began aloud to say:

" Ye Scottishmen spend a' our king's goud
   And a' our queenis fee."   30
" Ye lie, ye lie, ye liars loud,
   Fu' loud I hear ye lie.

" For I brought as mickle white monie
   As gane my men and me,
And I brought a half-fou o' gude red goud
   Out o'er the sea wi' me.

" Mak' ready, mak' ready, my merry men a',
   Our gude ship sails the morn."
" Now ever alake! my master dear,
   I fear a deadly storm.   40

17. *Weet.* Wet.   30. *Fee.* Wealth.
34. *Gane.* Sufficed.   35. *Fou.* Bushel.

" I saw the new moon late yestreen,
   Wi' the auld moon in her arm;
And if we gang to sea, master,
   I fear we'll come to harm."

They hadna sail'd upon the sea
   A day but barely three,
Till loud and boisterous grew the wind,
   And gurly grew the sea.

" O where will I get a gude sailor
   To tak' my helm in hand,   50
Till I gae up to the tall topmast
   To see if I can spy land? "

" O here am I a sailor gude,
   To tak' the helm in hand,
Till you gae up to the tall topmast,
   But I fear you'll ne'er spy land."

He hadna gane a step, a step,
   A step but barely ane,
When a bolt flew out o' our goodly ship,
   And the salt sea it came in.   60

" Gae fetch a web o' the silken claith,
   Anither o' the twine,
And wap them into our ship's side,
   And letna the sea come in."

48. *Gurly*. Rough.   61. *Claith*. Cloth.
        63. *Wap*. Throw quickly.

They fetched a web o' silken claith,
    Anither o' the twine,
And they wapped them into that gude
      ship's side,
    But still the sea cam' in.

O laith, laith were our gude Scots lords
    To weet their milk-white hands;   70
But lang ere a' the play was ower
    They wat their gouden bands.

O laith, laith were our gude Scots lords
    To weet their cork-heel'd shoon;
But lang ere a' the play was play'd
    They wat their hats aboon.

O lang, lang may the ladies sit
    Wi' their fans into their hand,
Before they see Sir Patrick Spens
    Come sailing to the land.   80

And lang, lang may the maidens sit
    Wi' their goud kaims in their hair
Awaiting for their ain dear loves,
    For them they'll see nae mair.

Half ower, half ower to Aberdour,
    It's fifty fathoms deep;
And there lies gude Sir Patrick Spens,
    Wi' the Scots lords at his feet.

OLD BALLAD.

69. *Laith.* Loth, unwilling.   74. *Shoon.* Shoes.
82. *Kaims.* Combs.

II. LORD ULLIN'S DAUGHTER

A CHIEFTAIN, to the Highlands bound,
  Cries, " Boatman, do not tarry,
And I'll give thee a silver pound
  To row us o'er the ferry."

" Now who be ye would cross Lochgyle,
  This dark and stormy water? "
" O, I'm the chief of Ulva's isle,
  And this Lord Ullin's daughter.

" And fast before her father's men
  Three days we've fled together,   10
For should he find us in the glen,
  My blood would stain the heather.

" His horsemen hard behind us ride;
  Should they our steps discover,
Then who will cheer my bonny bride
  When they have slain her lover? "

Out spoke the hardy Highland wight,
  " I'll go, my chief, I'm ready!
It is not for your silver bright;
  But for your winsome lady.   20

" And by my word! the bonny bird
   In danger shall not tarry;
So though the waves are raging white,
   I'll row you o'er the ferry."

By this the storm grew loud apace,
   The water-wraith was shrieking;
And in the scowl of Heaven each face
   Grew dark as they were speaking.

But still as wilder blew the wind,
   And as the night grew drearer,   30
Adown the glen rode armed men,
   Their trampling sounded nearer.

" O haste thee, haste! " the lady cries,
   " Though tempests round us gather;
I'll meet the raging of the skies,
   But not an angry father."

The boat has left a stormy land,
   A stormy sea before her—
When, oh! too strong, for human hand,
   The tempest gather'd o'er her.   40

And still they row'd amidst the roar
   Of waters fast prevailing;
Lord Ullin reach'd that fatal shore,
   His wrath was changed to wailing.

21. *Bird.* Maiden; confused with the old word " burd."

For sore dismay'd, through storm and shade,
  His child he did discover;
One lovely hand she stretch'd for aid,
  And one was round her lover.

" Come back! come back!" he cried in grief,
  " Across this stormy water;   50
And I'll forgive your Highland chief,
  My daughter! Oh, my daughter!"

'Twas vain: the loud waves lash'd the shore,
  Return or aid preventing.
The waters wild went o'er his child,
  And he was left lamenting.

THOMAS CAMPBELL.

III. THE BATTLE OF HOHENLINDEN

ON Linden when the sun was low,
All bloodless lay the untrodden snow,
And dark as winter was the flow
  Of Iser, rolling rapidly.

But Linden saw another sight,
When the drum beat at dead of night,
Commanding fires of death to light
  The darkness of her scenery.

By torch and trumpet fast arrayed,
Each warrior drew his battle-blade,   10
And furious every charger neighed,
   To join the dreadful revelry.

Then shook the hills with thunder riven,
Then rushed the steed to battle driven,
And louder than the bolts of Heaven,
   Far flashed the red artillery.

And redder yet those fires shall glow,
On Linden's hills of blood-stained snow;
And bloodier yet shall be the flow
   Of Iser, rolling rapidly.   20

'Tis morn! but scarce yon lurid sun
Can pierce the war-clouds, rolling dun,
Where furious Frank and fiery Hun
   Shout in their sulphurous canopy.

The combat deepens. On, ye brave
Who rush to glory, or the grave!
Wave, Munich! all thy banners wave
   And charge with all thy chivalry.

Few, few shall part, where many meet,
The snow shall be their winding-sheet,   30
And every turf beneath their feet
   Shall be a soldier's sepulchre.

               THOMAS CAMPBELL.

IV. ROSABELLE

O LISTEN, listen, ladies gay!
    No haughty feat of arms I tell;
Soft is the note and sad the lay
    That mourns the lovely Rosabelle.

" Moor, moor the barge, ye gallant crew!
    And, gentle lady, deign to stay!
Rest thee in Castle Ravensheuch,
    Nor tempt the stormy firth to-day.

" The blackening wave is edged with white;
    To inch and rock the sea-mews fly;   10
The fishers have heard the water-sprite,
    Whose screams forebode that wreck is nigh.

" Last night the gifted Seer did view.
    A wet shroud swathed round lady gay;
Then stay thee, Fair, in Ravensheuch;
    Why cross the gloomy firth to-day? "

" 'Tis not because Lord Lindesay's heir
    To-night at Roslin leads the ball,
But that my lady mother there
    Sits lonely in her castle hall.   20

10. *Inch.* Island.

" 'Tis not because the ring they ride,
    And Lindesay at the ring rides well,
But that my sire the wine will chide
    If 'tis not filled by Rosabelle."

O'er Roslin all that dreary night
    A wondrous blaze was seen to gleam;
'Twas broader than the watchfire's light,
    And redder than the bright moonbeam.

It glared on Roslin's castled rock,
    It ruddied all the copsewood glen;   30
'Twas seen from Dryden's groves of oak,
    And seen from cavern'd Hawthornden.

Seem'd all on fire that chapel proud,
    Where Roslin's chiefs uncoffin'd lie,
Each Baron, for a sable shroud,
    Sheath'd in his iron panoply.

Seem'd all on fire within, around,
    Deep sacristy and altar's pale;
Shone every pillar foliage-bound,
    And glimmer'd all the dead men's mail.   40

Blazed battlement and pinnet high,
    Blazed every rose-carved buttress fair:
So still they blaze, when fate is nigh
    The lordly line of high Saint Clair.

21. *Ring.* The ring used for tilting at.
38. *Pale.* Enclosure.

There are twenty of Roslin's barons bold
   Lie buried within that proud chapelle: 50
Each one the holy vault doth hold,
   But the sea holds lovely Rosabelle.

And each Saint Clair was buried there,
   With candle, with book, and with knell;
But the sea-caves rung, and the wild winds sung
   The dirge of lovely Rosabelle.

                    SIR WALTER SCOTT.

V. ALICE BRAND

MERRY it is in the good greenwood,
   When the mavis and merle are singing,
When the deer sweeps by, and the hounds are in cry,
   And the hunter's horn is ringing.

" O Alice Brand, my native land
   Is lost for love of you;
And we must hold by wood and wold,
   As outlaws wont to do.

" O Alice, 'twas all for thy locks so bright,
   And 'twas all for thine eyes so blue,   10
That on the night of our luckless flight,
   Thy brother bold I slew.

      2. *Mavis.* Thrush.   *Merle.* Blackbird.
      7. *Wold.* Open country.

" Now must I teach to hew the beech
   The hand that held the glaive,
For leaves to spread our lowly bed,
   And stakes to fence our cave.

" And for vest of pall, thy fingers small,
   That wont on harp to stray,
A cloak must shear from the slaughter'd deer,
   To keep the cold away."   20

" O Richard! if my brother died,
   'Twas but a fatal chance;
For darkling was the battle tried,
   And fortune sped the lance.

" If pall and vair no more I wear,
   Nor thou the crimson sheen,
As warm, we'll say, is the russet grey,
   As gay the forest-green.

" And Richard, if our lot be hard,
   And lost thy native land,   30
Still Alice has her own Richard,
   And he his Alice Brand."

.   .   .   .

'Tis merry, 'tis merry, in good greenwood,
   So blithe Lady Alice is singing:

14. *Glaive.* Sword.   17. *Pall.* Fine cloth.
25. *Vair.* Squirrel fur.
27. *Russet.* Homespun woollen cloth.

On the beech's pride, and oak's brown side,
  Lord Richard's axe is ringing.

Up spoke the moody Elfin King,
  Who won'd within the hill;
Like wind in the porch of a ruin'd church,
  His voice was ghostly shrill: 40

" Why sounds yon stroke on beech and oak,
  Our moonlight circle's screen?
Or who comes here to chase the deer,
  Beloved of our Elfin Queen?
Or who may dare on wold to wear
  The fairies' fatal green?

" Up, Urgan, up! to yon mortal hie,
  For thou wert christen'd man;
For cross or sign thou wilt not fly,
  For mutter'd word or ban.   50

" Lay on him the curse of the wither'd heart,
  The curse of the sleepless eye;
Till he wish and pray that his life would part,
  Nor yet find leave to die."

·   ·   ·   ·   ·   ·   ·

'Tis merry, 'tis merry, in good greenwood,
  Though the birds have still'd their singing;
The evening blaze doth Alice raise,
  And Richard is faggots bringing.

38. *Won'd.* Lived.

Up Urgan starts, that hideous dwarf,
 Before Lord Richard stands,   60
And, as he cross'd and bless'd himself,
" I fear not sign," quoth the grisly elf,
 " That is made with bloody hands."

But out then spoke she, Alice Brand,
 That woman void of fear:
" And if there's blood upon his hand,
 'Tis but the blood of deer."

" Now loud thou liest, thou bold of mood!
 It cleaves unto his hand,
The stain of thine own kindly blood, 70
 The blood of Ethert Brand."

Then forward stepp'd she, Alice Brand,
 And made the holy sign;
" And if there's blood on Richard's hand,
 A spotless hand is mine.

" And I conjure thee, Demon elf,
 By Him whom Demons fear,
To show us whence thou art thyself,
 And what thine errand here? "

 . . . .

" 'Tis merry, 'tis merry, in Fairy-land, 80
 When fairy birds are singing,
When the court doth ride by their monarch's side,
 With bit and bridle ringing:

   70. *Kindly.* Kindred.

" And gaily shines the Fairy-land—
  But all is glistening show,
Like the idle gleam that December's beam
  Can dart on ice and snow.

" And fading, like that varied gleam,
  Is our inconstant shape,
Who now like knight and lady seem,   90
  And now like dwarf and ape.

" It was between the night and day,
  When the Fairy King has power,
That I sunk down in a sinful fray,
And, 'twixt life and death, was snatched away
  To the joyless Elfin bower.

" But wist I of a woman bold,
  Who thrice my brow durst sign,
I might regain my mortal mould,
  As fair a form as thine."   100

She cross'd him once—she cross'd him twice—
  That lady was so brave;
The fouler grew his goblin hue,
  The darker grew the cave.

She crossed him thrice, that lady bold;
  He rose beneath her hand
The fairest knight on Scottish mould,
  Her brother, Ethert Brand!

Merry it is in good greenwood,
When the mavis and merle are singing, 110
But merrier were they in Dumfermline grey,
When all the bells were ringing.

SIR WALTER SCOTT.

VI. LOCHINVAR

LADY HERON'S SONG

O YOUNG Lochinvar is come out of the west,
Through all the wide Border his steed was the best;
And save his good broadsword, he weapons had none,
He rode all unarm'd and he rode all alone.
So faithful in love, and so dauntless in war,
There never was knight like the young Lochinvar.

He staid not for brake, and he stopp'd not for stone,
He swam the Eske river where ford there was none;
But ere he alighted at Netherby gate,
The bride had consented, the gallant came late: 10
For a laggard in love, and a dastard in war,
Was to wed the fair Ellen of brave Lochinvar.

So boldly he enter'd the Netherby Hall,
Among bride's-men, and kinsmen, and brothers, and all:
Then spoke the bride's father, his hand on his sword
(For the poor craven bridegroom said never a word),
" O come ye in peace here, or come ye in war,
Or to dance at our bridal, young Lord Lochinvar? "

" I long woo'd your daughter, my suit you denied—
Love swells like the Solway, but ebbs like its tide;　20
And now I am come, with this lost love of mine
To lead but one measure, drink one cup of wine.
There are maidens in Scotland more lovely by far,
That would gladly be bride to the young Lochinvar."

The bride kiss'd the goblet: the knight took it up,
He quaff'd off the wine, and he threw down the cup.
She look'd down to blush, and she look'd up to sigh,
With a smile on her lips, and a tear in her eye.
He took her soft hand, ere her mother could bar:
" Now tread we a measure! " said young Lochinvar.　30

So stately his form, and so lovely her face,
That never a hall such a galliard did grace;
While her mother did fret, and her father did fume,
And the bridegroom stood dangling his bonnet and
　　plume;
And the bride-maidens whisper'd " 'Twere better
　　by far,
To have match'd our fair cousin with young Loch-
　　invar."

One touch to her hand, and one word in her ear,
When they reach'd the hall-door, and the charger
　　stood near;
So light to the croupe the fair lady he swung,
So light to the saddle before her he sprung!　40

　　　32. *Galliard.* A lively dance.
　　　39. *Croupe.* Hind-quarters of a horse.

" She is won! we are gone, over bank, bush, and scaur;
They'll have fleet steeds that follow," quoth young
    Lochinvar.

There was mounting 'mong Græmes of the Netherby
    clan;
Forsters, Fenwicks, and Musgraves, they rode and
    they ran:
There was racing and chasing, on Cannobie Lee,
But the lost bride of Netherby ne'er did they see.
So daring in love, and so dauntless in war,
Have ye e'er heard of gallant like young Lochinvar?

                SIR WALTER SCOTT.

VII. THE HIGH TIDE ON THE COAST
OF LINCOLNSHIRE
(1571)

THE old mayor climbed the belfry tower,
    The ringers ran by two, by three;
" Pull, if ye never pulled before;
    Good ringers, pull your best," quoth he.
" Play uppe, play uppe, O Boston bells!
Ply all your changes, all your swells,
    Play uppe, ' The Brides of Enderby.' "

Men say it was a stolen tyde—
    The Lord that sent it, He knows all;
But in myne ears doth still abide   10
    The message that the bells let fall:

And there was nought of strange, beside
The flights of mews and peewits pied
By millions crouched on the old sea wall.

I sat and spun within the doore,
    My thread brake off, I raised myne eyes;
The level sun, like ruddy ore,
    Lay sinking in the barren skies,
And dark against day's golden death
She moved where Lindis wandereth,   20
My sonne's faire wife, Elizabeth.

"Cusha! Cusha! Cusha!" calling,
Ere the early dews were falling,
Farre away I heard her song.
"Cusha! Cusha!" all along
Where the reedy Lindis floweth,
    Floweth, floweth;
From the meads where melick groweth
Faintly came her milking song—

"Cusha! Cusha! Cusha!" calling,   30
"For the dews will soone be falling;
Leave your meadow grasses mellow
    Mellow, mellow;
Quit your cowslips, cowslips yellow;
Come uppe Whitefoot, come uppe Lightfoot,
Quit the stalks of parsley hollow,
    Hollow, hollow;
Come uppe Jetty, rise and follow,

        20. *Lindis.* The river Witham.
        28. *Melick.* A kind of grass.

From the clovers lift your head;
Come uppe Whitefoot, come uppe Lightfoot, 40
Come uppe Jetty, rise and follow,
Jetty, to the milking shed."

If it be long, ay, long ago,
   When I beginne to think howe long,
Againe I hear the Lindis flow,
   Swift as an arrowe, sharpe and strong;
And all the aire, it seemeth mee,
Bin full of floating bells (sayth shee),
That ring the tune of Enderby.

Alle fresh the level pasture lay   50
   And not a shadowe mote be seene,
Save where full fyve good miles away
   The steeple towered from out the greene;
And lo! the great bell farre and wide
Was heard in all the country side
That Saturday at eventide.

The swanherds where their sedges are
   Moved on in sunset's golden breath,
The shepherde lads I heard afarre,
   And my sonne's wife, Elizabeth;   60
Till floating o'er the grassy sea
Came downe that kyndly message free,
The " Brides of Mavis Enderby."

Then some looked uppe into the sky,
   And all along where Lindis flows
To where the goodly vessels lie,
   And where the lordly steeple shows,

They sayde, " And why should this thing be?
What danger lowers by land or sea?
They ring the tune of Enderby!   70

" For evil news from Mablethorpe,
    Of pyrate galleys warping downe;
For shippes ashore beyond the scorpe,
    They have not spared to wake the towne:
But while the west bin red to see,
And storms be none, and pyrates flee,
Why ring ' The Brides of Enderby'? "

I looked without, and lo! my sonne
    Came riding downe with might and main:
He raised a shout as he drew on,   80
    Till all the welkin rang again,
" Elizabeth! Elizabeth! "
(A sweeter woman ne'er drew breath
Than my sonne's wife, Elizabeth.)

" The olde sea wall (he cried) is downe,
    The rising tide comes on apace,
And boats adrift in yonder towne
    Go sailing uppe the market-place."
He shook as one that looks on death:
" God save you, mother! " straight he saith; 90
" Where is my wife, Elizabeth? "

" Good sonne, where Lindis winds away,
    With her two bairns I marked her long;
And ere yon bells beganne to play
    Afar I heard her milking-song."

B

He looked across the grassy lea,
To right, to left, " Ho Enderby! "
They rang " The Brides of Enderby! "

With that he cried and beat his breast;
    For lo! along the river's bed   100
A mighty eygre reared his crest,
    And uppe the Lindis raging sped.
It swept with thunderous noises loud;
Shaped like a curling snow-white cloud,
Or like a demon in a shroud.

And rearing Lindis backward pressed
    Shook all her trembling bankes amaine;
Then madly at the eygre's breast
    Flung uppe her weltering walls again.
Then bankes came down with ruin and rout—
Then beaten foam flew round about—   111
Then all the mighty floods were out.

So farre, so fast the eygre drave,
    The heart had hardly time to beat,
Before a shallow seething wave
    Sobbed in the grasses at our feet:
The feet had hardly time to flee
Before it brake against the knee,
And all the world was in the sea.

Upon the roofe we sate that night,   120
    The noise of bells went sweeping by;

101. *Eygre.* Tidal wave.

VIII. HERVÉ RIEL

I

On the sea and at the Hogue, sixteen hundred ninety-two,
  Did the English fight the French,—woe to France!
And, the thirty-first of May, helter-skelter through the blue,
Like a crowd of frightened porpoises a shoal of sharks pursue,
  Came crowding ship on ship to Saint-Malo on the Rance,
      With the English fleet in view.

II

'Twas the squadron that escaped, with the victor in full chase;
First and foremost of the drove, in his great ship, Damfreville;
      Close on him fled, great and small,
      Twenty-two good ships in all;   10
      And they signalled to the place
      " Help the winners of a race!
Get us guidance, give us harbour, take us quick,—or, quicker still,
      Here's the English can and will!"

III

Then the pilots of the place put out brisk and leapt on board;
  " Why, what hope or chance have ships like these to pass?"
          laughed they:
" Rocks to starboard, rocks to port, all the passage scarred and
          scored,—

5. *Rance.* The river which runs into the English Channel at St. Malo.

Shall the Formidable here, with her twelve and eighty guns,
   Think to make the river-mouth by the single narrow way,
Trust to enter—where 'tis ticklish for a craft of twenty tons, 20
        And with flow at full beside?
        Now, 'tis slackest ebb of tide.
        Reach the mooring? Rather say,
        While rock stands and water runs,
        Not a ship will leave the bay!"

IV

        Then was called a council straight.
        Brief and bitter the debate:
"Here's the English at our heels; would you have them take
      in tow
All that's left us of the fleet, linked together stern and bow,
        For a prize to Plymouth Sound?   30
        Better run the ships aground!"
        (Ended Damfreville his speech).
        "Not a minute more to wait!
        Let the Captains all and each
Shove ashore, then blow up, burn the vessels on the beach!
        France must undergo her fate.

V

        "Give the word!" But no such word
        Was ever spoke or heard;
For up stood, for out stepped, for in struck amid all these
—A Captain? A Lieutenant? A Mate—first, second, third? 40
        No such man of mark, and meet
        With his betters to compete!

But a simple Breton sailor pressed by Tourville for the fleet,
A poor coasting-pilot he, Hervé Riel the Croisickese.

VI

And " What mockery or malice have we here? " cries Hervé Riel:
" Are you mad, you Malouins? Are you cowards, fools, or rogues?
Talk to me of rocks and shoals, me who took the soundings, tell
On my fingers every bank, every shallow, every swell
'Twixt the offing here and Grève where the river disembogues?
Are you bought by English gold? Is it love the lying's for? 50
      Morn and eve, night and day,
      Have I piloted your bay,
Entered free and anchored fast at the foot of Solidor.
Burn the fleet and ruin France? That were worse than fifty
      Hogues!
Sirs, they know I speak the truth! Sirs, believe me there's a way!
      Only let me lead the line,
      Have the biggest ship to steer,
      Get this Formidable clear,
      Make the others follow mine,
And I lead them, most and least, by a passage I know well, 60
      Right to Solidor past Grève,
      And there lay them safe and sound;
      And if one ship misbehave,—
      Keel so much as grate the ground,
Why, I've nothing but my life,—here's my head!" cries Hervé
      Riel.

44. *Croisickese.* Native of Le Croisic, a village at the mouth of
the Loire.
46. *Malouins.* Natives of St. Malo.

VII

Not a minute more to wait.
" Steer us in, then, small and great!
Take the helm, lead the line, save the squadron!" cried its chief.
Captains, give the sailor place!
He is Admiral, in brief.—   70
Still the north-wind, by God's grace.
See the noble fellow's face
As the big ship, with a bound,
Clears the entry like a hound,
Keeps the passage, as its inch of way were the wide sea's profound!
See, safe thro' shoal and rock,
How they follow in a flock,
Not a ship that misbehaves, not a keel that grates the ground,
Not a spar that comes to grief!
The peril, see, is past.   80
All are harboured to the last,
And just as Hervé Riel hollas " Anchor!"—sure as fate,
Up the English come,—too late!

VIII

So, the storm subsides to calm:
They see the green trees wave
On the heights o'erlooking Grève.
Hearts that bled are staunched with balm.
" Just our rapture to enhance,
Let the English rake the bay,
Gnash our teeth and glare askance   90
As they cannonade away!

X. HOW THEY BROUGHT THE GOOD NEWS
FROM GHENT TO AIX

I SPRANG to the stirrup, and Joris, and he;
I galloped, Dirck galloped, we galloped all three;
" Good speed!" cried the watch, as the gate-bolts undrew;
" Speed!" echoed the wall to us galloping through;
Behind shut the postern, the lights sank to rest,
And into the midnight we galloped abreast.

Not a word to each other; we kept the great pace
Neck by neck, stride by stride, never changing our place;
I turned in my saddle and made its girths tight,
Then shortened each stirrup, and set the pique right,   · 10
Rebuckled the cheek-strap, chained slacker the bit,
Nor galloped less steadily Roland a whit.

'Twas moonset at starting; but while we drew near
Lokeren, the cocks crew and twilight dawned clear;
At Boom, a great yellow star came out to see;
At Düffeld, 'twas morning as plain as could be;
And from Mecheln church-steeple we heard the half-chime,
So Joris broke silence with, " Yet there is time!"

At Aërshot, up leaped of a sudden the sun,
And against him the cattle stood black every one,   20
To stare thro' the mist at us galloping past,
And I saw my stout galloper Roland at last,
With resolute shoulders, each butting away
The haze, as some bluff river headland its spray,

And his low head and crest, just one sharp ear bent back
For my voice, and the other pricked out on his track;
And one eye's black intelligence,—ever that glance
O'er its white edge at me, his own master, askance!
And the thick heavy spume-flakes which aye and anon
His fierce lips shook upwards in galloping on.   30

By Hasselt, Dirck groaned; and cried Joris, " Stay spur!
Your Roos galloped bravely, the fault's not in her,
We'll remember at Aix "—for one heard the quick wheeze
Of her chest, saw the stretched neck and staggering knees,
And sunk tail, and horrible heave of the flank,
As down on her haunches she shuddered and sank.

So we were left galloping, Joris and I,
Past Looz and past Tongres, no cloud in the sky!
The broad sun above laughed a pitiless laugh,
'Neath our feet broke the brittle bright stubble like chaff;   40
Till over by Dalhem a dome-spire sprang white,
And " Gallop," gasped Joris, " for Aix is in sight! "

" How they'll greet us! " and all in a moment his roan
Rolled neck and croup over, lay dead as a stone;
And there was my Roland to bear the whole weight
Of the news which alone could save Aix from her fate,
With his nostrils like pits full of blood to the brim,
And with circles of red for his eye-sockets' rim.

Then I cast loose my buffcoat, each holster let fall,
Shook off both my jack-boots, let go belt and all,   50

Stood up in the stirrup, leaned, patted his ear,
Called my Roland his pet-name, my horse without peer;
Clapped my hands, laughed and sang, any noise bad or good,
Till at length into Aix Roland galloped and stood.

And all I remember is, friends flocking round
As I sat with his head 'twixt my knees on the ground,
And no voice but was praising this Roland of mine,
As I poured down his throat our last measure of wine,
Which (the burgesses voted by common consent)   59
Was no more than his due who brought good news from Ghent.

ROBERT BROWNING.

XI. THE BALLAD OF AGINCOURT

FAIR stood the wind for France,
When we our sails advance,
Nor now to prove our chance
    Longer will tarry;
But putting to the main,
At Caux, the mouth of Seine,
With all his martial train
    Landed King Harry.

And taking many a fort,
Furnish'd in warlike sort,   10
Coming towards Agincourt
    In happy hour,
Skirmishing day by day
With those that stopp'd his way,
Whereas the General lay
    With all his power.

Which, in his height of pride,
King Henry to deride,
His ransome to provide
    Unto him sending: 20
Which he neglects the while,
As from a nation vile,
Yet with an angry smile
    Their fall portending.

And turning to his men,
Quoth our brave Henry then,
" Though they to one be ten,
    Be not amazèd:
Yet have we well begun;
Battles so bravely won   30
Have ever to the sun
    By fame been raisèd.

" And for my self (quoth he),
This my full rest shall be;
England ne'er mourn for me,
    Nor more esteem me;
Victor I will remain,
Or on this earth lie slain;
Never shall she sustain
    Loss to redeem me.   40

" Poitiers and Cressy tell,
When most their pride did swell,
Under our swords they fell;
    No less our skill is,
Than when our grandsire great,
Claiming the regal seat,
In many a warlike feat,
    Lopp'd the French Lilies."

The Duke of York so dread
The eager vaward led;   50
With the main Henry sped
    Among his henchmen.

34. *Rest.* Stake or venture; a gambling term.

Excester had the rear,
A braver man not there.
O Lord, how hot they were
    On the false Frenchmen!

They now to fight are gone,
Armour on armour shone,
Drum now to drum did groan,
    To hear was wonder;   60
That with the cries they make
The very earth did shake;
Trumpet to trumpet spake,
    Thunder to thunder.

Well it thine age became,
O noble Erpingham!
Which didst the signal frame
    To our hid forces;
When from a meadow by,
Like a storm, suddenly   70
The English archery
    Stuck the French horses.

The Spanish yew so strong,
Arrows a cloth-yard long,
That like to serpents stung,
    Piercing the weather:
None from his fellow starts,
But playing manly parts,
And like true English hearts
    Stuck close together.   80

When down their bows they threw,
And forth their bilbows drew,
And on the French they flew,
    No one was tardy.
Arms were from shoulders sent,
Scalps to the teeth were rent;
Down the French peasants went—
    Our men were hardy.

This while our noble King,
His broadsword brandishing,   90
Down the French host did fling,
    As to o'erwhelm it;
And many a deep wound lent,
His arms with blood besprent,
And many a cruel dent
    Bruisèd his helmet.

Glo'ster, that Duke so good,
Next of the royal blood,
For famous England stood
    With his brave brother: 100
Clarence in steel so bright,
Though but a maiden knight,
Yet in that furious fight,
    Scarce such another.

Warwick in blood did wade,
Oxford the foe invade,

82. *Bilbows.* Billhooks; properly, swords made at Bilbao.
86. *Scalps.* Skulls; the original sense.

And cruel slaughter made,
    Still as they ran up;
Suffolk his axe did ply,
Beaumont and Willoughby,   110
Bare them right doughtily,
    Ferrers and Fanhope.

Upon Saint Crispin's day
Fought was this noble fray,
Which fame did not delay
    To England to carry.
O! when shall Englishmen
With such acts fill a pen?
Or England breed again
    Such a King Harry?   120

             MICHAEL DRAYTON.

XII. THE BATTLE OF NASEBY

By Obadiah Bind-their-kings-in-chains-and-their-nobles-with-links-of-iron, Sergeant in Ireton's Regiment.

OH! wherefore come ye forth, in triumph from the North,
   With your hands, and your feet, and your raiment all red?
And wherefore doth your rout send forth a joyous shout?
   And whence be the grapes of the wine-press which ye tread?

Oh evil was the root, and bitter was the fruit,
   And crimson was the juice of the vintage that we trod;
For we trampled on the throng of the haughty and the strong
   Who sate in the high places, and slew the saints of God.

It was about the noon of a glorious day of June,
   That we saw their banners dance, and their cuirasses shine, 10
And the Man of Blood was there, with his long essenced hair,
   And Astley, and Sir Marmaduke, and Rupert of the Rhine.

Like a servant of the Lord, with his Bible and his sword,
   The General rode along us to form us to the fight,
When a murmuring sound broke out, and swell'd into a shout,
   Among the godless horsemen upon the tyrant's right.

And hark! like the roar of the billows on the shore,
   The cry of battle rises along their charging line!
For God! for the Cause! for the Church! for the Laws!
   For Charles, King of England, and Rupert of the Rhine! 20

The furious German comes, with his clarions and his drums,
　　His bravoes of Alsatia, and pages of Whitehall;
They are bursting on our flanks.　Grasp your pikes, close your
　　ranks;
　　For Rupert never comes but to conquer or to fall.

They are here! They rush on! We are broken! We are gone!
　　Our left is borne before them like stubble on the blast.
O Lord, put forth thy might! O Lord, defend the right!
　　Stand back to back, in God's name, and fight it to the last.

Stout Skippon hath a wound; the centre hath given ground;
　　Hark! hark!—What means the trampling of horsemen on our
　　rear?　　　　　　　　　　　　　　　　　　　　　　30
Whose banner do I see, boys? 'Tis he, thank God, 'tis he, boys.
　　Bear up another minute: brave Oliver is here.

Their heads all stooping low, their points all in a row,
　　Like a whirlwind on the trees, like a deluge on the dykes,
Our cuirassiers have burst on the ranks of the Accurst,
　　And at a shock have scattered the forest of his pikes.

Fast, fast, the gallants ride, in some safe nook to hide
　　Their coward heads, predestined to rot on Temple Bar;
And he—he turns, he flies:—shame on those cruel eyes
　　That bore to look on torture, and dare not look on war!　　40

Ho! comrades scour the plain; and, ere ye strip the slain
　　First give another stab to make your search secure;
Then shake from sleeves and pockets their broad-pieces and
　　lockets,
　　The tokens of the wanton, the plunder of the poor.

Fools! your doublets shone with gold, and your hearts were gay
    and bold,
  When you kissed your lily hands to your lemans to-day;
And to-morrow shall the fox, from her chambers in the rocks,
    Lead forth her tawny cubs to howl above the prey.

Where be your tongues that late mocked at heaven and hell and
    fate,
  And the fingers that once were so busy with your blades,   50
Your perfum'd satin clothes, your catches and your oaths,
    Your stage-plays and your sonnets, your diamonds and your
      spades?

Down, down, for ever down with the mitre and the crown,
    With the Belial of the Court and the Mammon of the Pope;
There is woe in Oxford halls; there is wail in Durham's stalls:
    The Jesuit smites his bosom: the Bishop rends his cope.

And She of the Seven Hills shall mourn her children's ills,
    And tremble when she thinks on the edge of England's sword;
And the Kings of earth in fear shall shudder when they hear
    What the hand of God hath wrought for the Houses and the
      Word.   60

LORD MACAULAY.

46. *Lemans.* Lovers.
51. *Catches.* Convivial songs.
57. *She of the Seven Hills.* Rome; *i.e.* the Papacy.
60. *Houses.* Parliament.

XIII. HAWKE

In seventeen hundred and fifty-nine,
    When Hawke came swooping from the West,
The French King's Admiral with twenty of the line,
    Was sailing forth, to sack us, out of Brest.
The ports of France were crowded, the quays of France a-hum
With thirty thousand soldiers marching to the drum,
For bragging time was over and fighting time was come
    When Hawke came swooping from the West.

'Twas long past noon of a wild November day
    When Hawke came swooping from the West;   10
He heard the breakers thundering in Quiberon Bay
    But he flew the flag for battle, line abreast.
Down upon the quicksands roaring out of sight
Fiercely beat the storm-wind, darkly fell the night,
But they took the foe for pilot and the cannon's glare for light
    When Hawke came swooping from the West.

The Frenchmen turned like a covey down the wind
    When Hawke came swooping from the West;
One he sank with all hands, one he caught and pinned,
    And the shallows and the storm took the rest.   20
The guns that should have conquered us they rusted on the shore,
The men that would have mastered us they drummed and marched
        no more,
For England was England, and a mighty brood she bore
    When Hawke came swooping from the West.

                              Sir Henry Newbolt.

XIV. AFTER BLENHEIM

IT was a summer evening,
　　Old Kaspar's work was done,
And he before his cottage door
　　Was sitting in the sun,
And by him sported on the green
His little grandchild Wilhelmine.

She saw her brother Peterkin,
　　Roll something large and round,
Which he beside the rivulet
　　In playing there had found;   10
He came to ask what he had found
That was so large and smooth and round.

Old Kaspar took it from the boy,
　　Who stood expectant by;
And then the old man shook his head,
　　And with a natural sigh—
" 'Tis some poor fellow's skull," said he,
" Who fell in the great victory.

" I find them in the garden,
　　For there's many here about;   20
And often when I go to plough
　　The ploughshare turns them out!
For many thousand men," said he,
" Were slain in that great victory."

" Now tell us what 'twas all about,"
    Young Peterkin he cries:
And little Wilhelmine looks up
    With wonder-waiting eyes;
" Now tell us all about the war,
And what they fought each other for."   30

" It was the English," Kaspar cried,
    " Who put the French to rout;
But what they fought each other for
    I could not well make out.
But everybody said," quoth he,
" That 'twas a famous victory.

" My father lived at Blenheim then,
    Yon little stream hard by;
They burnt his dwelling to the ground,
    And he was forced to fly;   40
So with his wife and child he fled,
Nor had he where to rest his head.

" With fire and sword the country round
    Was wasted far and wide,
And many a childing mother then
    And new-born baby died;
But things like that, you know, must be
At every famous victory.

" They say it was a shocking sight,
    After the field was won;   50
For many thousand bodies here
    Lay rotting in the sun;

But things like that, you know, must be
After a famous victory.

" Great praise the Duke of Marlbro' won,
 And our good Prince Eugene."
" Why, 'twas a very wicked thing! "
 Said little Wilhelmine.
" Nay, nay, my little girl," quoth he,
" It was a famous victory.

" And everybody praised the Duke
 Who this great fight did win."
" But what good came of it at last? "
 Quoth little Peterkin.
" Why, that I cannot tell," said he,
" But 'twas a famous victory."

ROBERT SOUTHEY.

XV. THE BURIAL OF SIR JOHN MOORE

NOT a drum was heard, not a funeral note,
 As his corpse to the rampart we hurried;
Not a soldier discharged his farewell shot,
 O'er the grave where our hero we buried.

We buried him darkly, at dead of night,
 The sods with our bayonets turning;
By the struggling moonbeam's misty light,
 And the lantern dimly burning.

No useless coffin enclosed his breast,
   Not in sheet nor in shroud we wound him;   10
But he lay like a warrior taking his rest,
   With his martial cloak around him.

Few and short were the prayers we said,
   And we spoke not a word of sorrow;
But we steadfastly gazed on the face that was dead,
   And we bitterly thought of the morrow.

We thought, as we hollowed his narrow bed,
   And smoothed down his lonely pillow,
That the foe and the stranger would tread o'er his head,
   And we far away on the billow!   20

Lightly they'll talk of the spirit that's gone,
   And o'er his cold ashes upbraid him;—
But little he'll reck, if they let him sleep on,
   In a grave where a Briton has laid him.

But half of our heavy task was done
   When the clock struck the hour for retiring;
And we heard the distant and random gun
   That the foe was sullenly firing.

Slowly and sadly we laid him down,
   From the field of his fame fresh and gory;   30
We carved not a line, and we raised not a stone—
   But we left him alone with his glory!

                        CHARLES WOLFE.

XVI. ADMIRAL HOSIER'S GHOST

As near Porto-Bello[1] lying
　On the gently swelling flood,
At midnight with streamers flying,
　Our triumphant navy rode;
There while Vernon sat all-glorious
　From the Spaniard's late defeat;
And his crews, with shouts victorious,
　Drank success to England's fleet:

On a sudden shrilly sounding,
　Hideous yells and shrieks were heard:　10
Then each heart with fear confounding,
　A sad troop of ghosts appear'd,
All in dreary hammocks shrouded,
　Which for winding-sheets they wore,
And with looks by sorrow clouded,
　Frowning on that hostile shore.

[1] The case of Hosier, which is here so pathetically represented, was briefly this. In April, 1726, that commander was sent with a strong fleet into the Spanish West Indies, to block up the galleons in the ports of that country, or should they presume to come out, to seize and carry them into England: he accordingly arrived at the Bastimentos near Porto-Bello, but being restricted by his orders from obeying the dictates of his courage, lay inactive on that station until he became the jest of the Spaniards: he afterwards moved to Carthagena, and continued cruising in these seas, till far the greater part of his men perished deplorably by the diseases of that unhealthy climate. This brave man, seeing his best officers and men thus daily swept away, his ships exposed to inevitable destruction, and himself made the sport of the enemy, is said to have died of a broken heart.—RICHARD GLOVER.

On them gleam'd the moon's wan lustre,
    When the shade of Hosier brave
His pale bands was seen to muster,
    Rising from their wat'ry grave: 20
O'er the glimm'ring wave he hied him,
    Where the Burford rear'd her sail,
With three thousand ghosts beside him,
    And in groans did Vernon hail.

" Heed, O heed, our fatal story,
    I am Hosier's injur'd ghost.
You, who now have purchas'd glory
    At this place where I was lost;
Though in Porto-Bello's ruin
    You now triumph free from fears,   30
When you think on our undoing,
    You will mix your joy with tears.

" See these mournful spectres, sweeping
    Ghastly o'er this hated wave,
Whose wan cheeks are stain'd with weeping;
    These were English captains brave:
Mark those numbers pale and horrid,
    Those were once my sailors bold,
Lo! each hangs his drooping forehead,
    While his dismal tale is told.   40

" I, by twenty sail attended,
    Did this Spanish town affright:
Nothing then its wealth defended
    But my orders not to fight:

O! that in this rolling ocean
   I had cast them with disdain,
And obey'd my heart's warm motion,
   To have quell'd the pride of Spain.

" For resistance I could fear none,
   But with twenty ships had done   50
What thou, brave and happy Vernon,
   Hast achiev'd with six alone.
Then the Bastimentos never
   Had our foul dishonour seen,
Nor the sea the sad receiver
   Of this gallant train had been.

" Thus, like thee, proud Spain dismaying,
   And her galleons leading home,
Though condemn'd for disobeying,
   I had met a traitor's doom;   60
To have fall'n, my country crying
   He has play'd an English part,
Had been better far than dying
   Of a griev'd and broken heart.

" Unrepining at thy glory,
   Thy successful arms we hail;
But remember our sad story,
   And let Hosier's wrongs prevail.
Sent in this foul clime to languish,
   Think what thousands fell in vain,   70
Wasted with disease and anguish,
   Not in glorious battle slain.

" Hence, with all my train attending
    From their oozy tombs below,
Through the hoary foam ascending,
    Here I feed my constant woe:
Here the Bastimentos viewing,
    We recall our shameful doom,
And our plaintive cries renewing,
    Wander through the midnight gloom.   80

" O'er these waves for ever mourning
    Shall we roam depriv'd of rest,
If to Britain's shores returning,
    You neglect my just request.
After this proud foe subduing,
    When your patriot friends you see,
Think on vengeance for my ruin,
    And for England sham'd in me."

                          RICHARD GLOVER.

XVII.—THE CAPTAIN

A LEGEND OF THE NAVY

HE that only rules by terror
    Doeth grievous wrong.
Deep as Hell I count his error.
    Let him hear my song.
Brave the Captain was: the seamen
    Made a gallant crew.

Gallant sons of English freemen,
  Sailors bold and true.
But they hated his oppression,
  Stern he was and rash;   10
So for every light transgression
  Doom'd them to the lash.
Day by day more harsh and cruel
  Seem'd the Captain's mood.
Secret wrath like smother'd fuel
  Burnt in each man's blood.
Yet he hoped to purchase glory,
  Hoped to make the name
Of his vessel great in story,
  Wheresoe'er he came.   20
So they past by capes and islands,
  Many a harbour-mouth,
Sailing under palmy highlands
  Far within the South.
On a day when they were going
  O'er the lone expanse,
In the north, her canvas flowing,
  Rose a ship of France.
Then the Captain's colour heighten'd,
  Joyful came his speech: 30
But a cloudy gladness lighten'd
  In the eyes of each.
" Chase," he said: the ship flew forward,
  And the wind did blow;
Stately, lightly, went she Nor'ward,
  Till she near'd the foe.
Then they look'd at him they hated,

c

Had what they desired:
Mute with folded arms they waited—
  Not a gun was fired.   40
But they heard the foeman's thunder
  Roaring out their doom;
All the air was torn in sunder,
  Crashing went the boom,
Spars were splinter'd, decks were shatter'd,
  Bullets fell like rain;
Over mast and deck were scatter'd
  Blood and brains of men.
Spars were splinter'd; decks were broken:
  Every mother's son—   50
Down they dropt—no word was spoken—
  Each beside his gun.
On the decks as they were lying,
  Were their faces grim.
In their blood, as they lay dying,
  Did they smile on him.
Those in whom he had reliance
  For his noble name
With one smile of still defiance
  Sold him unto shame.   60
Shame and wrath his heart confounded,
  Pale he turn'd and red,
Till himself was deadly wounded,
  Falling on the dead.
Dismal error! Fearful slaughter!
  Years have wander'd by,
Side by side beneath the water
  Crew and Captain lie;

There the sunlit ocean tosses
    O'er them mouldering,   70
And the lonely seabird crosses
    With one waft of the wing.

LORD TENNYSON.

XVIII. THE LADY OF SHALOTT

PART I

ON either side the river lie
Long fields of barley and of rye,
That clothe the wold and meet the sky;
And thro' the field the road runs by
    To many-tower'd Camelot;
And up and down the people go,
Gazing where the lilies blow,
Round an island there below,
    The island of Shalott.

Willows whiten, aspens quiver,   10
Little breezes dusk and shiver
Thro' the wave that runs for ever
By the island in the river
    Flowing down to Camelot.
Four gray walls, and four gray towers,
Overlook a space of flowers,
And the silent isle imbowers
    The Lady of Shalott.

7. Blow. Bloom.

By the margin, willow-veil'd,
Slide the heavy barges trail'd   20
By slow horses; and unhail'd
The shallop flitteth silken-sail'd
    Skimming down to Camelot:
But who hath seen her wave her hand?
Or at the casement seen her stand?
Or is she known in all the land,
    The Lady of Shalott?

Only reapers, reaping early
In among the bearded barley,
Hear a song that echoes cheerly   30
From the river winding clearly,
    Down to tower'd Camelot:
And by the moon the reaper weary,
Piling sheaves in uplands airy,
Listening, whispers, " 'Tis the fairy
    Lady of Shalott."

PART II

There she weaves by night and day
A magic web with colours gay,
She has heard a whisper say,
A curse is on her if she stay   40
    To look down to Camelot.
She knows not what the curse may be,
And so she weaveth steadily,
And little other care hath she,
    The Lady of Shalott.

    22. *Shallop.* Small boat; sloop.

And moving thro' a mirror clear
That hangs before her all the year,
Shadows of the world appear.
There she sees the highway near
    Winding down to Camelot: 50
There the river eddy whirls,
And there the surly village churls,
And the red cloaks of market girls,
    Pass onward from Shalott.

Sometimes a troop of damsels glad,
An abbot on an ambling pad,
Sometimes a curly shepherd-lad,
Or long-hair'd page in crimson clad,
    Goes by to tower'd Camelot;
And sometimes thro' the mirror blue 60
The knights come riding two and two:
She hath no loyal knight and true,
    The Lady of Shalott.

But in her web she still delights
To weave the mirror's magic sights,
For often thro' the silent nights
A funeral, with plumes and lights
    And music, went to Camelot:
Or when the moon was overhead,
Came two young lovers lately wed; 70
" I am half sick of shadows," said
    The Lady of Shalott.

56. *Pad*. Road horse; pad means path.

Part III

A bow-shot from her bower-eaves,
He rode between the barley-sheaves,
The sun came dazzling thro' the leaves,
And flamed upon the brazen greaves
    Of bold Sir Lancelot.
A red-cross knight for ever kneel'd
To a lady in his shield,
That sparkled on the yellow field,   80
    Beside remote Shalott.

The gemmy bridle glitter'd free,
Like to some branch of stars we see
Hung in the golden Galaxy.
The bridle bells rang merrily
    As he rode down to Camelot:
And from his blazon'd baldric slung
A mighty silver bugle hung,
And as he rode his armour rung,
    Beside remote Shalott.   90

All in the blue unclouded weather
Thick-jewell'd shone the saddle leather,
The helmet and the helmet-feather
Burn'd like one burning flame together,
    As he rode down to Camelot.
As often thro' the purple night,
Below the starry clusters bright,
Some bearded meteor, trailing light,
    Moves over still Shalott.

87. *Blazon'd baldric.* Belt adorned with heraldic devices.

His broad clear brow in sunlight glow'd; 100
On burnish'd hooves his war-horse trode;
From underneath his helmet flow'd
His coal-black curls as on he rode,
    As he rode down to Camelot.
From the bank and from the river
He flash'd into the crystal mirror,
" Tirra lirra," by the river
    Sang Sir Lancelot.

She left the web, she left the loom,
She made three paces thro' the room, 110
She saw the water-lily bloom,
She saw the helmet and the plume,
    She look'd down to Camelot.
Out flew the web and floated wide;
The mirror crack'd from side to side;
" The curse is come upon me," cried
    The Lady of Shalott.

PART IV

In the stormy east-wind straining,
The pale yellow woods were waning,
The broad stream in his banks complaining,
Heavily the low sky raining 121
    Over tower'd Camelot;
Down she came and found a boat
Beneath a willow left afloat,
And round about the prow she wrote
    The Lady of Shalott.

And down the river's dim expanse
Like some bold seër in a trance,
Seeking all his own mischance—
With a glassy countenance   130
    Did she look to Camelot.
And at the closing of the day
She loosed the chain, and down she lay;
The broad stream bore her far away,
    The Lady of Shalott.

Lying robed in snowy white
That loosely flew to left and right—
The leaves upon her falling light—
Thro' the noises of the night
    She floated down to Camelot: 140
And as the boat-head wound along
The willowy hills and fields among,
They heard her singing her last song,
    The Lady of Shalott.

Heard a carol, mournful, holy,
Chanted loudly, chanted lowly,
Till her blood was frozen slowly,
And her eyes were darken'd wholly,
    Turn'd to tower'd Camelot;
For ere she reach'd upon the tide   150
The first house by the water-side,
Singing in her song she died,
    The Lady of Shalott.

Under tower and balcony,
By garden-wall and gallery,

A gleaming shape she floated by,
Dead-pale between the houses high,
 Silent into Camelot.
Out upon the wharfs they came,
Knight and burgher, lord and dame,   160
And round the prow they read her name,
 The Lady of Shalott.

Who is this? and what is here?
And in the lighted palace near
Died the sound of royal cheer;
And they cross'd themselves for fear,
 All the knights at Camelot:
But Lancelot mused a little space;
He said, " She has a lovely face;
God in His mercy lend her grace,   170
 The Lady of Shalott."

        LORD TENNYSON.

XIX. THE FORSAKEN MERMAN

COME, dear children, let us away;
Down and away below!
Now my brothers call from the bay,
Now the great winds shoreward blow,
Now the salt tides seaward flow;
Now the wild white horses play,
Champ and chafe and toss in the spray.
Children dear, let us away!
This way, this way!

Call her once before you go—   10
Call once yet!
In a voice that she will know:
" Margaret! Margaret! "
Children's voices should be dear
(Call once more) to a mother's ear:
Children's voices, wild with pain—
Surely she will come again!
Call her once and come away;
This way, this way!
" Mother dear, we cannot stay.   20
The wild white horses foam and fret."
Margaret! Margaret!

Come, dear children, come away down;
Call no more!
One last look at the white-wall'd town,
And the little grey church on the windy shore,
Then come down!
She will not come though you call all day;
Come away, come away!

Children dear, was it yesterday   30
We heard the sweet bells over the bay?
In the caverns where we lay,
Through the surf and through the swell,
The far-off sound of a silver bell?
Sand-strewn caverns, cool and deep,
Where the winds are all asleep;
Where the spent lights quiver and gleam,
Where the salt weed sways in the stream.

Where the sea-beasts, rang'd all round,
Feed in the ooze of their pasture-ground;   40
Where the sea-snakes coil and twine,
Dry their mail and bask in the brine;
Where great whales come sailing by,
Sail and sail, with unshut eye,
Round the world for ever and aye?
When did music come this way?
Children dear, was it yesterday?

Children dear, was it yesterday
(Call yet once) that she went away?
Once she sate with you and me,   50
On a red gold throne in the heart of the sea,
And the youngest sate on her knee.
She comb'd its bright hair, and she tended it well,
When down swung the sound of a far-off bell.
She sigh'd, she look'd up through the clear green sea;
She said: " I must go, for my kinsfolk pray
In the little grey church on the shore to-day.
'Twill be Easter-time in the world—ah me!
And I lose my poor soul, Merman, here with thee."
I said: " Go up, dear heart, through the waves;   60
Say thy prayer, and come back to the kind sea-caves!"
She smil'd, she went up through the surf in the bay.
Children dear, was it yesterday?

    Children dear, were we long alone?
" The sea grows stormy, the little ones moan;
Long prayers," I said, " in the world they say;
Come," I said, and we rose through the surf in the bay.
We went up the beach, by the sandy down

Where the sea-stocks bloom, to the white-wall'd town;
Through the narrow pav'd streets, where all was still,
To the little grey church on the windy hill.　　　　71
From the church came a murmur of folk at their prayers,
But we stood without in the cold blowing airs.
We climb'd on the graves, on the stones worn with rains,
And we gaz'd up the aisle through the small leaded panes.
She sate by the pillar; we saw her clear:
" Margaret, hist! come quick, we are here!
Dear heart," I said, " we are long alone.
The sea grows stormy, the little ones moan."
But, ah, she gave me never a look,　　　　　　　80
For her eyes were seal'd to the holy book!
Loud prays the priest; shut stands the door.
Come away, children, call no more!
Come away, come down, call no more!

　Down, down, down!
Down to the depths of the sea!
She sits at her wheel in the humming town,
Singing most joyfully.
Hark what she sings: " O joy, O joy,
For the humming street, and the child with its toy!　90
For the priest, and the bell, and the holy well;
For the wheel where I spun,
And the blessed light of the sun."
And so she sings her fill,
Singing most joyfully,
Till the spindle falls from her hand,
And the whizzing wheel stands still.
She steals to the window, and looks at the sand,

And over the sand at the sea;
And her eyes are set in a stare; 100
And anon there breaks a sigh,
And anon there drops a tear,
From a sorrow-clouded eye,
And a heart sorrow-laden,
A long, long sigh;
For the cold strange eyes of a little Mermaiden,
And the gleam of her golden hair.

Come away, away, children;
Come children, come down!
The hoarse wind blows coldly: 110
Lights shine in the town.
She will start from her slumber
When gusts shake the door;
She will hear the winds howling,
Will hear the waves roar.
We shall see, while above us
The waves roar and whirl,
A ceiling of amber,
A pavement of pearl.
Singing, " Here came a mortal, 120
But faithless was she!
And alone dwell for ever
The kings of the sea."

But, children, at midnight,
When soft the winds blow,
When clear falls the moonlight,
When spring-tides are low:
When sweet airs come seaward

From heaths starr'd with broom;
And high rocks throw mildly   130
On the blanch'd sands a gloom:
Up the still, glistening beaches,
Up the creeks we will hie,
Over banks of bright seaweed
The ebb-tide leaves dry.
We will gaze, from the sand-hills,
At the white, sleeping town;
At the church on the hillside—
And then come back down.
Singing, " There dwells a lov'd one,   140
But cruel is she!
She left lonely for ever
The kings of the sea."

MATTHEW ARNOLD.

XX. JASON'S PLOUGHING

Jason, with his comrades the Minyæ, had sailed in the *Argo* from Thessaly to Colchis on the Black Sea or Euxine, to win from King Æetes the famous Golden Fleece. Jason was set a task. He must first yoke Æetes' brazen, fire-breathing bulls, plough with them the War God's field, sow it with serpents' teeth, and garner the strange crop that should grow up. The king's daughter Medea, a potent enchantress, through love for Jason gave him certain charms and directions for their use.

BUT down the hall the king passed, who did hold
Medea's hand, and on a car of gold
They mounted, drawn anigh the carven door,
And spearmen of the Colchians went before
And followed after, and the Minyæ
Set close together followed solemnly,
Headed by Jason, at the heels of these.

So passed they through the streets and palaces
Thronged with much folk, and o'er the bridges passed,
And to the open country came at last,   10
Nor there went far, but turning to the right,
Into a close they came, where there were dight
Long galleries about the fateful stead,
Built all of marble fair and roofed with lead,
And carved about with stories of old time,
Framed all about with golden lines of rhyme.
Moreover, midmost was an image made
Of mighty Mars who maketh kings afraid,
That looked down on an altar builded fair,
Wherefrom already did a bright fire glare   20
And made the hot air glassy with its heat.
    So in the gallery did the king take seat
With fair Medea, and the Colchians stood
Hedging the twain in with a mighty wood
Of spears and axes, while the Minyæ
Stood off a space the fated things to see.
    Ugly and rugged was that spot of ground,
And with an iron wall was closed around,
And at the further end a monstrous cage
Of iron bars, shut in the stupid rage   30
Of those two beasts, and therefrom ever came
The flashing and the scent of sulphurous flame,
As with their brazen, clangorous bellowing
They hailed the coming of the Colchian king;
Nor was there one of the seafaring men
But trembled, gazing on the deadly pen,
But Jason only, who before the rest

12. *Dight.* Constructed.   13. *Stead.* Enclosure.

Shone like a star, having upon his breast
A golden corslet from the treasury
Of wise King Phineus by the doubtful sea,   40
By an Egyptian wrought who would not stay
At Salmydessa more than for a day,
But on that day the wondrous breast-plate wrought,
Which, with good will and strong help, Jason bought;
And from that treasury his golden shoe
Came, and his thighs the king's gift covered too;
But on his head his father's helm was set,
Wreathed round with bay leaves, and his sword lay yet
Within the scabbard, while his ungloved hand
Bore nought within it but an olive wand.   50

     Now King Æetes well beholding him,
Fearless of mien and so unmatched of limb,
Trembled a little in his heart as now
He bade the horn-blowers the challenge blow,
But thought, "What strength can help him, or what art,
Or which of all the Gods be on his part?"
Impious, who knew not through what doubtful days,
E'en from his birth, and perilous rough ways
Juno had brought him safely, nor indeed
Of his own daughter's quivering lips took heed,   60
And restless hands wherein the God so wrought,
The wise man seeing her had known her thought.

     Now Jason, when he heard the challenge blow,
Across the evil fallow 'gan to go
With face beyond its wont in nowise pale,
Nor footsteps faltering, if that might avail
The doomed man aught; so to the cage he came,
Whose bars now glowed red hot with spouted flame,

In many a place; nor doubted any one
Who there beheld him that his days were done, 70
Except his love alone, and even she,
Sickening with doubt and terror, scarce could see
The hero draw the brazen bolt aside
And throw the glowing wicket open wide.

But he alone, apart from his desire,
Stood unarmed, facing those two founts of fire,
Yet feared not aught, for hope and fear were dead
Within his heart, and utter hardihead
Had Juno set there; but the awful beasts
Beholding now the best of all their feasts, 80
Roared in their joy and fury, till from sight
They and the prince were hidden by the white,
Thick rolling clouds of sulphurous pungent smoke,
Through which upon the blinded man they broke.
But when within a yard of him they came,
Baffled they stopped, still bellowing, and the flame
Still spouting out from nostril and from mouth,
As from some island mountain in the south
The trembling mariners behold it cast;
But still to right and left of him it passed, 90
Breaking upon him as cool water might,
Nor harming more, except that from his sight
All corners of the cage were hidden now,
Nor knew he where to seek the brazen plough;
As to and fro about the quivering cage
The monsters rushed in blind and helpless rage.
But as he doubted, to his eyes alone
Within the place a golden light outshone,
Scattering the clouds of smoke, and he beheld

Once more the Goddess who his head upheld   100
In rough Anaurus on that other tide;
She, smiling on him, beckoned, and 'gan glide
With rosy feet across the fearful floor,
Breathing cool odours round her, till a door
She opened to him in the iron wall,
Through which he passed, and found a grisly stall
Of iron still, and at one end of it,
By glimmering lamps with greenish flame half lit,
Beheld the yoke and shining plough he sought;
Which, seizing straight, by mighty strength he brought
Unto the door, nor found the Goddess there,   111
Who in the likeness of a damsel fair,
Colchian Metharma, through the spearmen passed,
Bearing them wine, and causeless terror cast
Into their foolish hearts, nor spared to go
And 'mid the close seafaring ranks to sow
Good hope of joyful ending, and then stood
Behind the maid unseen, and brought the blood
Back to her cheeks and trembling lips and wan,
With thoughts of things unknown to maid and man.

    Meanwhile upon the foreheads of the twain   121
Had Jason cast the yoke with little pain,
And drove them now with shouts out through the door
Which in such guise ne'er had they passed before,
For never were they made the earth to till,
But rather, feeding fat, to work the will
Of some all-knowing man; but now they went
Like any peasant's beasts, tamed by the scent
Of those new herbs Medea's hand had plucked,
Whose roots from evil earth strange power had sucked.

Now in the open field did Jason stand   131
And to the plough-stilts set his unused hand,
And down betwixt them lustily he bent;
Then the bulls drew, and the bright ploughshare sent
The loathly fallow up on the right side,
Whilst o'er their bellowing shrilly Jason cried:
" Draw nigh, O King, and thy new ploughman see,
Then mayst thou make me shepherd, too, to thee;
Nor doubt thou, doing so, from out thy flock
To lose but one, who ne'er shall bring thee stock, 140
Or ram or ewe, nor doubt the grey wolf, King,
Wood-haunting bear, dragon, or such like thing.
Ah the straight furrow! how it mindeth me
Of the smooth parting of the land-locked sea
Over against Eubœa, and this fire
Of the fair altar where my joyful sire
Will pour out wine to Neptune when I come
Not empty-handed back unto my home."
Such mocks he said; but when the sunlight broke
Upon his armour through the sulphurous smoke, 150
And showed the lengthening furrow cutting through
The ugly fallow as anigh they drew,
The joyful Minyæ gave a mighty shout;
But pale the king sat with brows knit for doubt,
Muttering: " Whose counsel hast thou taken, then,
To do this thing, which not the best of men
Would do unholpen of some sorcery?
Whoso it is, wise were he now to die
Ere yet I know him, since for many a day
Vainly for death I hope to hear him pray."   160

145. *Fire.* Supply " reminds me."

Meanwhile, askance Medea eyed the king,
Thinking nought safe until that everything
Was finished in the Colchian land, and she
No more beheld its shores across the sea;
But he, beholding her pale visage, thought
Grief like to his such paleness on her brought,
And turning to her, said: " How pale thou art!
Let not this first foil go unto thine heart
Too deeply, since thou knowest certainly,
One way or other this vain fool must die."   170
" Father," she said, " a doubt is on me still,
Some God this is come here our wealth to spill;
Nor is this first thing easier than the rest."
Then stammering, she said: " Were it not best
To give him that which he must have at last,
Before he slays us? " But Æetes cast
A sharp glance at her, and a pang shot through
His weary heart as half the truth he knew.
But for one moment, and he made reply
In passionate words: " Then, daughter, let me die!
And, ere I die, behold thee led along   181
A wretched slave to suffer grief and wrong
In far-off lands, and Æa at thy back
Nought but a huge flame hiding woe and wrack,
Before from out my willing open hand
This wonder, and the safeguard of my land
A God shall take; and such this man is not.
What! dost thou think because his eyes are hot
On tender maidens he must be a God?
Or that because firmly this field he trod   190

172. *Spill.* Destroy.   183. *Æa.* The old name of Colchis.

Well-fenced with magic? Were he like to me,
Grey-haired and lean, what Godhead wouldst thou see
In such an one? Hold, then, thy peace of this,
And thou shalt see thy God full widely miss
The mark he aims at, when from out the earth
Spring up those brothers of an evil birth."

  And therewithal he gazed at her, and thought
To see the rosy flush by such words brought
Across her face; as in the autumn eve,
Just as the sun's last half begins to leave   200
The shivering world, both east and west are red.—
But calm and pale she turned about her head,
And said: " My father, neither were these words
My words, nor would I struggle with my lords;
Thou art full wise; whatso thine heart would have
That do, and heed me not, who fain would save
This glory of my kingdom and of thee.
But now look up, and soothly thou shalt see
Mars' acre tilled: the field is ready then,
Bid them bring forth the seed that beareth men."   210

  Again with her last words the shouts out-broke
From the seafarers, for, beside the yoke,
Before Mars' altar did Prince Jason stand,
Holding the wand of olive in his hand,
And on the new-turned furrow shone the sun
Behind him, and his half-day's work was done.

  And now another marvel: for, behold,
As at the furrow's end he slacked his hold
Upon the plough-stilts, all the bellowing
Wherewith the beasts had made the grim close ring,
Fell suddenly, and all the fire died   221

That they were wont erewhile to scatter wide
From mouth and nostril, and their loins and knees
Stiffened, and they grew nought but images
Lifelike but lifeless, wonderful but dead,
Such as he makes, who many a day hath fed
His furnace with the beechwood, when the clay
Has grown beneath his deft hands day by day
And all is ready for the casting, then
Such things as these he makes for royal men.   230

But 'mid the shouts turned Jason to the king,
And said: " Fair sir, behold a wondrous thing,
And since these beasts have been content to stay
Before Mars' altar, from this very day
His should they be if they were mine to give."

" O Jason," said the king, " well mayst thou live
For many a day, since thou this deed hast done,
But for the Gods, not unto any one
Will I give gifts; but let them take from me
What once they gave, if so the thing must be.   240
But do thou take this sack from out my hand
And cast its seed about the new-tilled land,
And watch the issue; and keep words till then,
I counsel thee, O luckiest of men."

Then Jason took the sack, and with it went
About that field new turned, and broadcast sent
The white teeth scattering, but or ere he came
Back to the altar, and the flickering flame,
He heard from 'neath the earth a muttered sound
That grew and grew, till all that piece of ground   250
Swelled into little hillocks, like as where
A stricken field was foughten, but that there

Quiet the heroes' bones lie underneath
The quivering grasses and the dusky heath;
But now these heaps the labouring earth upthrew
About Mars' acre, ever greater grew,
And still increased the noise, till none could hear
His fellow speak, and paleness and great fear
Fell upon all; and Jason only stood
As stands the stout oak in the poplar wood   260
When winds are blowing.
                                   Then he saw the mounds
Bursten asunder, and the muttered sounds
Changed into loud strange shouts and warlike clang,
As with freed feet at last the earth-born sprang
On to the tumbling earth, and the sunlight
Shone on bright arms clean ready for the fight.
    But terribly they showed, for through the place
Not one there was but had his staring face,
With great wide eyes, and lips in a set smile,
Turned full on Jason, who, for a short while,   270
Forgot indeed Medea's warning word,
And from its golden sheath half drew his sword,
But then, remembering all, cried valiantly:
" New born ye are—new slain too shall ye be,
Take this, and round about it read your doom,
And bid them make new dwellings in the tomb,
Wherefrom ye came, nor ever should have passed."
    Therewith the ball among the host he cast,
Standing to watch what next the folk would do.
But he the ball had smitten turned unto   280
The one who stood by him and like a cup
Shattered his head; then the next lifted up

His axe and slew the slayer, and straightway
Among the rest began a deadly fray.

   No man gave back a foot, no breathing space
One took or gave within that dreadful place,
But where the vanquished stood there was he slain,
And straight the conquering arm was raised again
To meet its match and in its turn to fall,
No tide was there of fainting and recall,   290
No quivering pennon o'er their heads to flit,
Nor name or eager shout called over it,
No groan of pain, and no despairing cry
From him who knows his time has come to die,
But passionless each bore him in that fight,
Scarce otherwise than as a smith might smite
On sounding iron or bright glittering brass.

   So, little by little, did the clamour pass
As one by one each fell down in his place,
Until at last, midmost the bloody space,   300
One man was left, alive but wounded sore,
Who, staring round about and seeing no more
His brothers' spears against him, fixed his eyes
Upon the queller of those mysteries.
Then dreadfully they gleamed, and with no word,
He tottered towards him with uplifted sword.
But scarce he made three paces down the field,
Ere chill death reached his heart, and on his shield
Clattering he fell. So satiate of fight
Quickly the earth-born were, and their delight   310
With what it fed on perished, and one hour
Ripened the deadly fruit of that fell flower.
                                   WILLIAM MORRIS.

XXI. THE HEALING OF CONALL CARNACH

O'ER Slieve Few, with noiseless tramping through the heavy-
     drifted snow,
Beälcu, Connacia's champion, in his chariot tracks the foe;
And anon far off discerneth, in the mountain-hollow white,
Slinger Keth and Conall Carnach mingling, hand to hand in fight.

Swift the charioteer his coursers urged across the wintry glade;
Hoarse the cry of Keth and hoarser seem'd to come demanding
     aid;
But through wreath and swollen runnel ere the car could reach
     anigh,
Keth lay dead, and mighty Conall bleeding lay at point to die.

Whom beholding spent and pallid, Beälcu exulting cried,
"Oh thou ravening wolf of Uladh, where is now thy northern
     pride?   10
What can now that crest audacious, what that pale defiant brow,
Once the bale-star of Connacia's ravaged fields, avail thee now?"

"Taunts are for reviling woman"; faintly Conall made reply:
"Wouldst thou play the manlier foeman, end my pain and let me
     die.

     2. *Beälcu*. Pronounced Bayal-kú.   *Connacia*. Connaught.
     7. *Wreath*. Snow-drift.   10. *Uladh*. Ulster; pronounced Ullad.

Neither deem thy blade dishonour'd that with Keth's a deed it
    share,
For the foremost two of Connaught feat enough and fame to
    spare."

"No, I will not! bard shall never in Dunseverick Hall make
    boast
That to quell one northern riever needed two of Croghan's host.
But because that word thou'st spoken, if but life enough remains,
Thou shalt hear the wives of Croghan clap their hands above thy
    chains.   20

"Yea, if life enough but linger, that the leech may make thee
    whole,
Meet to satiate the anger that beseems a warrior's soul,
Best of leech-craft I'll purvey thee; make thee whole as healing
    can;
And in single combat slay thee, Connaught man to Ulster man."

Binding him in five-fold fetter, wrists and ankles, wrists and neck,
To his car's uneasy litter Beälcu upheaved the wreck
Of the broken man and harness; but he started with amaze
When he felt the northern war-mace, what a weight it was to
    raise.

Westward then through Breiffny's borders, with his captive and
    his dead,
Track'd by bands of fierce applauders, wives and shrieking widows,
    sped;   30

      17. *Dunseverick.* Carnach's castle in Antrim.

And the chain'd heroic carcass on the fair-green of Moy Slaught
Casting down, proclaim'd his purpose, and bade Lee the leech be
    brought.

Lee, the gentle-faced physician, from his herb-plot came, and said,
" Healing is with God's permission: health for life's enjoyment
    made:
And though I mine aid refuse not, yet, to speak my purpose plain,
I the healing art abuse not, making life enure to pain.

" But assure me, with the sanction of the mightiest oath ye know,
That in case, in this contention, Conall overcome his foe,
Straight departing from the tourney by what path the chief shall
    choose,
He is free to take his journey unmolested to the Fews.   40

" Swear me further, while at healing in my charge the hero lies,
None shall through my fences stealing, work him mischief or
    surprise;
So, if God the undertaking but approve, in six months' span
Once again my art shall make him meet to stand before a man."

Crom their god they then attested, Sun and Wind for guarantees,
Conall Carnach unmolested by what exit he might please,
If the victor, should have freedom to depart Connacia's bounds;
Meantime, no man should intrude him entering on the hospice
    grounds.

Then his burden huge receiving in the hospice-portal, Lee,
Stiffen'd limb by limb relieving with the iron fetter key,

As a crumpled scroll unroll'd him, groaning deep, till laid at
    length,   50
Wondering gazers might behold him, what a tower he was of
    strength.

Spake the sons to one another, day by day, of Beälcu—
" Get thee up and spy, my brother, what the leech and northman
    do."
" Lee, at mixing of a potion: Conall, yet in no wise dead,
As on reef of rock the ocean, tosses wildly on his bed."

" Spy again with cautious peeping; what of Lee and Conall
    now?"
" Conall lies profoundly sleeping; Lee beside with placid brow."
" And to-day?"   " To-day he's risen; pallid as his swathing
    sheet,
He has left his chamber's prison, and is walking on his feet."

" And to-day?"   " A ghostly figure on his javelin propp'd he
    goes."   60
" And to-day?"   " A languid vigour through his larger gesture
    shows."
" And to-day?"   " The blood renewing mantles all his clear
    cheek through."
" Would thy vow had room for rueing, rashly-valiant Beälcu!"

So with herb and healing balsam, ere the second month was past,
Life's additions smooth and wholesome circling through his
    members vast,
As you've seen a sere oak burgeon under summer showers and dew,
Conall, under his chirurgeon, fill'd and flourish'd, spread and grew.

" I can bear the sight no longer: I have watch'd him moon by
    moon:
Day by day the chief grows stronger: giant-strong he will be soon.
O my sire, rash-valiant warrior! but that oaths have built the
    wall,   70
Soon these feet should leap the barrier: soon this hand thy fate
    forestall."

" Brother, have the wish thou'st utter'd; we have sworn, so let
    it be;
But although our feet be fetter'd, all the air is left us free.
Dying Keth with vengeful presage did bequeath thee sling and
    ball,
And the sling may send its message where thy vagrant glances
    fall.

" Forbaid was a master-slinger: Maev, when in her bath she sank,
Felt the presence of his finger from the further Shannon bank;
For he threw by line and measure, practising a constant cast
Daily in secluded leisure, till he reach'd the mark at last.

" Keth achieved a warrior's honour, though 'twas 'mid a woman's
    band,   80
When he smote the amorous Conor bowing from his distant stand.
Fit occasion will not fail ye: in the leech's lawn below,
Conall at the fountain daily drinks within an easy throw."

" Wherefore cast ye at the apple, sons of mine, with measured
    aim ? "
" He who in the close would grapple, first the distant foe should
    maim.

And since Keth, his death-balls casting, rides no more the ridge
    of war,
We, against our summer hosting, train us for his vacant car."

" Wherefore to the rock repairing, gaze ye forth, my children, tell."
" 'Tis a stag we watch for snaring, that frequents the leech's well."
" I will see this stag, though, truly, small may be my eye's
    delight."   90
And he climbed the rock where fully lay the lawn exposed to sight.

Conall to the green well-margin came at dawn and knelt to drink,
Thinking how a noble virgin by a like green fountain's brink
Heard his own pure vows one morning far away and long ago:
All his heart to home was turning; and his tears began to flow.

Clean forgetful of his prison, steep Dunseverick's windy tower
Seem'd to rise in present vision, and his own dear lady's bower.
Round the sheltering knees they gather, little ones of tender
    years,—
Tell us, mother, of our father—and she answers but with tears.

Twice the big drops plash'd the fountain. Then he rose, and
    turning round,   100
As across a breast of mountain sweeps a whirlwind o'er the ground
Raced in athlete-feats amazing, swung the war-mace, hurl'd the
    spear;
Beälcu, in wonder gazing, felt the pangs of deadly fear.

Had it been a fabled griffin, suppled in a fasting den,
Flash'd its wheeling coils to heaven o'er a wreck of beasts and men,
Hardly had the dreadful prospect bred his soul more dire alarms;
Such the fire of Conall's aspect, such the stridor of his arms!

107. *Stridor.* Clank.

" This is fear," he said, " that never shook these limbs of mine
    till now.
Now I see the mad endeavour; now I mourn the boastful vow.
Yet 'twas righteous wrath impell'd me; and a sense of manly
    shame   110
From his naked throat withheld me when 'twas offer'd to my aim.

" Now I see his strength excelling: whence he buys it: what he
    pays:
'Tis a God who has a dwelling in the fount, to whom he prays.
Thither came he weeping, drooping, till the Well-God heard his
    prayer:
Now behold him, soaring, swooping, as an eagle through the air.

" O thou God, by whatsoever sounds of awe thy name we know,
Grant thy servant equal favour with the stranger and the foe!
Equal grace, 'tis all I covet; and if sacrificial blood
Win thy favour, thou shalt have it on thy very well-brink, God!

" What and though I've given pledges not to cross the leech's
    court?   120
Not to pass his sheltering hedges, meant I to his patient's hurt.
Thy dishonour meant I never: never meant I to forswear
Right divine of prayer wherever Power divine invites to prayer.

" Sun that warm'st me, Wind that fann'st me, ye that guarantee
    the oath,
Make no sign of wrath against me: tenderly ye touch me both.
Yea, then, through his fences stealing ere to-morrow's sun shall rise,
Well-God! on thy margin kneeling, I will offer sacrifice."

" Brother, rise, the skies grow ruddy: if we yet would save our sire,
Rests a deed courageous, bloody, wondering ages shall admire:
Hie thee to the spy-rock's summit; ready there thou'lt find the
    sling;   130
Ready there the leaden plummet; and at dawn he seeks the
    spring."

Ruddy dawn had changed to amber: radiant as the yellow day,
Conall issuing from his chamber, to the fountain took his way:
There, athwart the welling water, like a fallen pillar, spread,
Smitten by the bolt of slaughter, lay Connacia's champion dead.

Call the hosts! convene the judges! cite the dead man's children
    both!—
Said the judges, " He gave pledges; Sun and Wind; and broke
    the oath,
And they slew him: so we've written: let his sons attend our
    words."

      .   .   .   .   .   .

" Both, by sudden frenzy smitten, fell at sunrise on their swords."

Then the judges, " Ye who punish man's prevaricating vow, 140
Needs not further to admonish: contrite to their will we bow,
All our points of promise keeping: safely let the chief go forth."
Conall to his chariot leaping, turned his coursers to the north:

In the Sun that swept the valleys, in the Wind's encircling flight,
Recognising holy allies, guardians of the Truth and Right;
While, before his face, resplendent with a firm faith's candid ray,
Dazzled troops of foes attendant, bow'd before him on his way.

But the calm physician, viewing where the white neck join'd the
    ear,
Said, " It is a slinger's doing: Sun nor Wind was actor here.
Yet till God vouchsafe more certain knowledge of his sovereign
    will,   150
Better deem the mystic curtain hides their wonted demons still.

" Better so, perchance, than living in a clearer light, like me,
But believing where perceiving, bound in what I hear and see;
Force and change in constant sequence, changing atoms, change-
    less laws;
Only in submissive patience waiting access to the Cause."

                                  SIR SAMUEL FERGUSON.

XXII. THE DEATH OF CUCHULAIN

A MAN came slowly from the setting sun,
To Forgail's daughter, Emer, in her dun,
And found her dyeing cloth with subtle care,
And said, casting aside his draggled hair:
" I am Aleel, the swineherd, whom you bid
Go dwell upon the sea cliffs, vapour-hid;
But now my years of watching are no more."

Then Emer cast the web upon the floor,
And stretching out her arms, red with the dye,
Parted her lips with a loud sudden cry.   10

Looking on her, Aleel, the swineherd, said:
" Not any god alive, nor mortal dead,
Has slain so mighty armies, so great kings,
Nor won the gold that now Cuchulain brings."

" Why do you tremble thus from feet to crown? "
Aleel, the swineherd, wept and cast him down
Upon the web-heaped floor, and thus his word:
" With him is one sweet-throated like a bird."

" Who bade you tell these things? " and then she
            cried   20
To those about, " Beat him with thongs of hide

Cuchulain. Pronounce Coohóolan.
2. *Dun.* Fortified residence of a chief.

And drive him from the door." And thus it was;
And where her son, Finmole, on the smooth grass
Was driving cattle, came she with swift feet,
And called out to him, " Son, it is not meet
That you stay idling here with flock and herds."

" I have long waited, mother, for those words;
But wherefore now? "
      " There is a man to die;
You have the heaviest arm under the sky." 30

" My father dwells among the sea-worn bands,
And breaks the ridge of battle with his hands."

" Nay, you are taller than Cuchulain, son."

" He is the mightiest man in ship or dun."

" Nay, he is old and sad with many wars,
And weary of the crash of battle cars."

" I only ask what way my journey lies,
For God, who made you bitter, made you wise."

" The Red Branch kings a tireless banquet keep,
Where the sun falls into the Western deep, 40
Go there, and dwell on the green forest rim;
But tell alone your name and house to him
Whose blade compels, and bid them send you one
Who has a like vow from their triple dun."

Between the lavish shelter of a wood
And the grey tide, the Red Branch multitude
Feasted, and with them old Cuchulain dwelt,
And his young dear one close beside him knelt,
And gazed upon the wisdom of his eyes,
More mournful than the depth of starry skies,   50
And pondered on the wonder of his days;
And all around the harp-string told his praise,
And Concobar, the Red Branch king of kings,
With his own fingers touched the brazen strings.

At last Cuchulain spake, " A young man strays
Driving the deer along the woody ways.
I often hear him singing to and fro,
I often hear the sweet sound of his bow.
Seek out what man he is."
                                        One went and came.
" He bade me let all know he gives his name   60
At the sword point, and bade me bring him one
Who had a like vow from our triple dun."

" I only of the Red Branch hosted now,"
Cuchulain cried, " have made and keep that vow."

After short fighting in the leafy shade,
He spake to the young man, " Is there no maid
Who loves you, no white arms to wrap you round,
Or do you long for the dim sleepy ground,
That you come here to meet this ancient sword? "

53. *Concobar.* Connor.

"The dooms of men are in God's hidden hoard."   70

"Your head a while seemed like a woman's head
That I loved once."
                  Again the fighting sped,
But now the war rage in Cuchulain woke,
And through the other's shield his long blade
    broke,
And pierced him.
              "Speak before your breath is done."

"I am Finmole, mighty Cucnulain's son."

"I put you from your pain. I can no more."

While day its burden on to evening bore,
With head bowed on his knees Cuchulain stayed;
Then Concobar sent that sweet-throated maid,   80
And she, to win him, his grey hair caressed:
In vain her arms, in vain her soft white breast.
Then Concobar, the subtlest of all men,
Ranking his Druids round him ten by ten,
Spake thus, "Cuchulain will dwell there and brood,
For three days more in dreadful quietude,
And then arise, and raving slay us all.
Go, cast on him delusions magical,
That he may fight the waves of the loud sea."
And ten by ten under a quicken tree,   90
The Druids chaunted, swaying in their hands
Tall wands of alder and white quicken wands.

      90. *Quicken tree*. Mountain-ash; rowan.

In three days' time, Cuchulain with a moan
Stood up, and came to the long sands alone:
For four days warred he with the bitter tide;
And the waves flowed above him, and he died.

W. B. YEATS.

XXIII. LA BELLE DAME SANS MERCI

I

"O WHAT can ail thee, knight-at-arms,
Alone and palely loitering?
The sedge has wither'd from the lake,
And no birds sing.

II

O what can ail thee, knight-at-arms,
So haggard and so woe-begone?
The squirrel's granary is full,
And the harvest's done.

III

I see a lily on thy brow
With anguish moist and fever dew;   10
And on thy cheek a fading rose
Fast withereth too."

IV

"I met a lady in the meads,
Full beautiful—a faery's child;
Her hair was long, her foot was light,
And her eyes were wild.

V

I made a garland for her head,
  And bracelets too, and fragrant zone;
She look'd at me as she did love,
  And made sweet moan.   20

VI

I set her on my pacing steed,
  And nothing else saw all day long,
For sideways would she bend, and sing
  A faery's song.

VII

She found me roots of relish sweet,
  And honey wild, and manna dew,
And sure in language strange she said,
  ' I love thee true.'

VIII

She took me to her elfin grot,
  And there she wept and sigh'd full sore,   30
And there I shut her wild wild eyes
  With kisses four.

IX

And there she lulled me asleep,
  And there I dream'd—ah! woe betide!
The latest dream I ever dream'd
  On the cold hill side.

X

I saw pale kings and princes too,
  Pale warriors, death-pale were they all;
Who cry'd—" La Belle Dame Sans Merci
  Thee hath in thrall! "

                                  40

XI

I saw their starv'd lips in the gloam
  With horrid warning gaped wide,
And I awoke, and found me here
  On the cold hill side.

XII

And this is why I sojourn here,
  Alone and palely loitering,
Though the sedge is withered from the lake,
  And no birds sing."

                         JOHN KEATS.

XXIV. LOVE

ALL thoughts, all passions, all delights,
  Whatever stirs this mortal frame,
All are but ministers of Love,
    And feed his sacred flame.

Oft in my waking dreams do I
Live o'er again that happy hour,
When midway on the mount I lay,
    Beside the ruined tower.

The moonshine, stealing o'er the scene
Had blended with the lights of eve;   10
And she was there, my hope, my joy,
    My own dear Genevieve!

She leant against the armèd man,
The statue of the armèd knight;
She stood and listened to my lay,
    Amid the lingering light.

Few sorrows hath she of her own.
My hope! my joy! my Genevieve!
She loves me best, whene'er I sing
    The songs that make her grieve.   20

I played a soft and doleful air,
I sang an old and moving story—
An old rude song, that suited well
    That ruin wild and hoary.

She listened with a flitting blush,
With downcast eyes and modest grace;
For well she knew, I could not choose
    But gaze upon her face.

I told her of the Knight that wore
Upon his shield a burning brand;   30
And that for ten long years he wooed
    The Lady of the Land.

I told her how he pined: and ah!
The deep, the low, the pleading tone
With which I sang another's love,
    Interpreted my own.

She listened with a flitting blush,
With downcast eyes, and modest grace;
And she forgave me, that I gazed
    Too fondly on her face!   40

But when I told the cruel scorn
That crazed that bold and lovely Knight,
And that he crossed the mountain-woods,
    Nor rested day nor night;

That sometimes from the savage den,
And sometimes from the darksome shade,
And sometimes starting up at once
    In green and sunny glade,—

There came and looked him in the face
An angel beautiful and bright;   50
And that he knew it was a Fiend,
    This miserable Knight!

And that unknowing what he did,
He leaped amid a murderous band,
And saved from outrage worse than death
    The Lady of the Land!

And how she wept, and clasped his knees;
And how she tended him in vain—
And ever strove to expiate
    The scorn that crazed his brain;—   60

And that she nursed him in a cave;
And how his madness went away,
When on the yellow forest-leaves
    A dying man he lay;—

His dying words—but when I reached
That tenderest strain of all the ditty,
My faltering voice and pausing harp
    Disturbed her soul with pity!

All impulses of soul and sense
Had thrilled my guileless Genevieve;   70
The music and the doleful tale,
    The rich and balmy eve;

And hopes, and fears that kindle hope,
An undistinguishable throng,
And gentle wishes long subdued,
    Subdued and cherished long!

She wept with pity and delight,
She blushed with love, and virgin shame;
And like the murmur of a dream,
    I heard her breathe my name.   80

Her bosom heaved—she stepped aside,
As conscious of my look she stepped—
Then suddenly, with timorous eye
    She fled to me and wept.

She half enclosed me with her arms,
She pressed me with a meek embrace;
And bending back her head, looked up,
    And gazed upon my face.

'Twas partly love, and partly fear,
And partly 'twas a bashful art,
That I might rather feel, than see,   90
    The swelling of her heart.

I calmed her fears, and she was calm,
And told her love with virgin pride;
And so I won my Genevieve,
    My bright and beauteous Bride.

                                    S. T. COLERIDGE.

XXV. THE SENSITIVE PLANT

PART I

A SENSITIVE PLANT in a garden grew,
And the young winds fed it with silver dew,
And it opened its fan-like leaves to the light,
And closed them beneath the kisses of Night.

And the Spring arose on the garden fair,
Like the Spirit of Love felt everywhere;
And each flower and herb on Earth's dark breast
Rose from the dreams of its wintry rest.

But none ever trembled and panted with bliss
In the garden, the field, or the wilderness,   10
Like a doe in the noontide with love's sweet want
As the companionless Sensitive Plant.

The snowdrop, and then the violet,
Arose from the ground with warm rain wet,
And their breath was mixed with fresh odour, sent
From the turf, like the voice and the instrument

Then the pied wind-flowers and the tulip tall,
And narcissi, the fairest among them all,
Who gaze on their eyes in the stream's recess,
Till they die of their own dear loveliness;   20

And the Naïad-like lily of the vale,
Whom youth makes so fair and passion so pale
That the light of its tremulous bells is seen
Through their pavilions of tender green;

And the hyacinth purple, and white, and blue,
Which flung from its bells a sweet peal anew
Of music so delicate, soft, and intense,
It was felt like an odour within the sense;

And the rose like a nymph to the bath addressed,
Which unveiled the depth of her glowing breast,   30
Till, fold after fold, to the fainting air
The soul of her beauty and love lay bare:

And the wand-like lily, which lifted up,
As a Mænad, its moonlight-coloured cup,
Till the fiery star, which is its eye,
Gazed through clear dew on the tender sky;

And the jessamine faint, and the sweet tuberose,
The sweetest flower for scent that blows;
And all rare blossoms from every clime
Grew in that garden in perfect prime.   40

And on the stream whose inconstant bosom
Was pranked, under boughs of embowering blossom,
With golden and green light, slanting through
Their heaven of many a tangled hue,

Broad water-lilies lay tremulously,
And starry river-buds glimmered by,
And around them the soft stream did glide and dance
With a motion of sweet sound and radiance.

And the sinuous paths of lawn and of moss,
Which led through the garden along and across,   50
Some open at once to the sun and the breeze,
Some lost among bowers of blossoming trees,

Were all paved with daisies and delicate bells
As fair as the fabulous asphodels,
And flow'rets which, drooping as day drooped too,
Fell into pavilions, white, purple, and blue,
To roof the glow-worm from the evening dew.

And from this undefilèd Paradise
The flowers (as an infant's awakening eyes
Smile on its mother, whose singing sweet   60
Can first lull, and at last must awaken it),

When Heaven's blithe winds had unfolded them,
As mine-lamps enkindle a hidden gem,
Shone smiling to Heaven, and every one
Shared joy in the light of the gentle sun;

For each one was interpenetrated
With the light and the odour its neighbour shed,
Like young lovers whom youth and love make dear
Wrapped and filled by their mutual atmosphere.

But the Sensitive Plant which could give small fruit 70
Of the love which it felt from the leaf to the root,
Received more than all, it loved more than ever,
Where none wanted but it, could belong to the giver:

For the Sensitive Plant has no bright flower;
Radiance and odour are not its dower;
It loves, even like Love, its deep heart is full,
It desires what it has not, the Beautiful!

The light winds which from unsustaining wings
Shed the music of many murmurings;
The beams which dart from many a star   80
Of the flowers whose hues they bear afar;

The plumèd insects swift and free,
Like golden boats on a sunny sea,
Laden with light and odour, which pass
Over the gleam of the living grass;

The unseen clouds of the dew, which lie
Like fire in the flowers till the sun rides high,
Then wander like spirits among the spheres,
Each cloud faint with the fragrance it bears;

The quivering vapours of dim noontide,   90
Which like a sea o'er the warm earth glide,
In which every sound, and odour, and beam,
Move, as reeds in a single stream;

Each and all like ministering angels were
For the Sensitive Plant sweet joy to bear,
Whilst the lagging hours of the day went by
Like windless clouds o'er a tender sky.

And when evening descended from Heaven above,
And the Earth was all rest, and the air was all love,
And delight, though less bright, was far more deep, 100
And the day's veil fell from the world of sleep,

And the beasts, and the birds, and the insects were
      drowned
In an ocean of dreams without a sound;
Whose waves never mark, though they ever impress
The light sand which paves it, consciousness;

(Only overhead the sweet nightingale
Ever sang more sweet as the day might fail,
And snatches of its Elysian chant
Were mixed with the dreams of the Sensitive Plant);—

The Sensitive Plant was the earliest   110
Upgathered into the bosom of rest;
A sweet child weary of its delight,
The feeblest and yet the favourite,
Cradled within the embrace of Night.

PART II

There was a Power in this sweet place,
An Eve in this Eden; a ruling Grace
Which to the flowers, did they waken or dream,
Was as God is to the starry scheme.

A Lady, the wonder of her kind,
Whose form was upborne by a lovely mind   120
Which, dilating, had moulded her mien and motion
Like a sea-flower unfolded beneath the ocean,

Tended the garden from morn to even:
And the meteors of that sublunar Heaven,
Like the lamps of the air when Night walks forth,
Laughed round her footsteps up from the Earth!

She had no companion of mortal race,
But her tremulous breath and her flushing face
Told, whilst the morn kissed the sleep from her eyes,
That her dreams were less slumber than Paradise: 130

As if some bright Spirit for her sweet sake
Had deserted Heaven while the stars were awake,
As if yet around her he lingering were,
Though the veil of daylight concealed him from her.

Her step seemed to pity the grass it pressed;
You might hear by the heaving of her breast,
That the coming and going of the wind
Brought pleasure there and left passion behind.

And wherever her aëry footstep trod,
Her trailing hair from the grassy sod   140
Erased its light vestige, with shadowy sweep,
Like a sunny storm o'er the dark green deep.

I doubt not the flowers of that garden sweet
Rejoiced in the sound of her gentle feet;
I doubt not they felt the spirit that came
From her glowing fingers through all their frame.

She sprinkled bright water from the stream
On those that were faint with the sunny beam;
And out of the cups of the heavy flowers
She emptied the rain of the thunder-showers.   150

She lifted their heads with her tender hands,
And sustained them with rods and osier-bands;
If the flowers had been her own infants, she
Could never have nursed them more tenderly.

And all killing insects and gnawing worms,
And things of obscene and unlovely forms,
She bore, in a basket of Indian woof,
Into the rough woods far aloof,—

In a basket, of grasses and wild-flowers full,
The freshest her gentle hands could pull   160
For the poor banished insects, whose intent,
Although they did ill, was innocent.

But the bee and the beamlike ephemeris
Whose path is the lightning's, and soft moths that kiss
The sweet lips of the flowers, and harm not, did she
Make her attendant angels be.

And many an antenatal tomb,
Where butterflies dream of the life to come,
She left clinging round the smooth and dark
Edge of the odorous cedar bark.   170

This fairest creature from earliest Spring
Thus moved through the garden ministering
All the sweet season of Summertide,
And ere the first leaf looked brown—she died!

Part III

Three days the flowers of the garden fair,
Like stars when the moon is awakened, were,
Or the waves of Baiæ, ere luminous
She floats up through the smoke of Vesuvius.

And on the fourth, the Sensitive Plant
Felt the sound of the funeral chant,   180
And the steps of the bearers heavy and slow,
And the sobs of the mourners, deep and low;

The weary sound and the heavy breath,
And the silent motions of passing death,
And the smell, cold, oppressive, and dank,
Sent through the pores of the coffin-plank;

The dark grass, and the flowers among the grass,
Were bright with tears as the crowd did pass;
From their sighs the wind caught a mournful tone,
And sate in the pines, and gave groan for groan.

The garden, once fair, became cold and foul, 191
Like the corpse of her who had been its soul,
Which at first was lovely as if in sleep,
Then slowly changed, till it grew a heap
To make men tremble who never weep.

Swift Summer into the Autumn flowed,
And frost in the mist of the morning rode,
Though the noonday sun looked clear and bright,
Mocking the spoil of the secret night.

The rose-leaves, like flakes of crimson snow, 200
Paved the turf and the moss below.
The lilies were drooping, and white, and wan,
Like the head and the skin of a dying man.

And Indian plants, of scent and hue
The sweetest that ever were fed on dew,
Leaf by leaf, day after day,
Were massed into the common clay.

And the leaves, brown, yellow, and grey, and red,
And white with the whiteness of what is dead,
Like troops of ghosts on the dry wind passed; 210
Their whistling noise made the birds aghast.

And the gusty winds waked the wingèd seeds,
Out of their birthplace of ugly weeds,
Till they clung round many a sweet flower's stem,
Which rotted into the earth with them.

The water-blooms under the rivulet
Fell from the stalks on which they were set;
And the eddies drove them here and there,
As the winds did those of the upper air.

Then the rain came down, and the broken stalks   220
Were bent and tangled across the walks;
And the leafless network of parasite bowers
Massed into ruin; and all sweet flowers.

Between the time of the wind and the snow
All loathliest weeds began to grow,
Whose coarse leaves were splashed with many a speck,
Like the water-snake's belly and the toad's back.

And thistles, and nettles, and darnels rank,
And the dock, and henbane, and hemlock dank,
Stretched out its long and hollow shank,   230
And stifled the air till the dead wind stank.

And plants, at whose names the verse feels loath,
Filled the place with a monstrous undergrowth,
Prickly, and pulpous, and blistering, and blue,
Livid, and starred with a lurid dew.

Their moss rotted off them, flake by flake,
Till the thick stalk stuck like a murderer's stake,
Where rags of loose flesh yet tremble on high,
Infecting the winds that wander by.

And agarics, and fungi, with mildew and mould   240
Started like mist from the wet ground cold;
Pale, fleshy, as if the decaying dead
With a spirit of growth had been animated!

Spawn, weeds, and filth, a leprous scum,
Made the running rivulet thick and dumb,
And at its outlet flags huge as stakes
Dammed it up with roots knotted like water-snakes.

And hour by hour, when the air was still,
The vapours arose which have strength to kill;
At morn they were seen, at noon they were felt,   250
At night they were darkness no star could melt.

And unctuous meteors from spray to spray
Crept and flitted in broad noonday
Unseen; every branch on which they alit
By a venomous blight was burned and bit.

The Sensitive Plant, like one forbid,
Wept, and the tears within each lid
Of its folded leaves, which together grew,
Were changed to a blight of frozen glue.

For the leaves soon fell, and the branches soon 260
By the heavy axe of the blast were hewn;
The sap shrank to the root through every pore
As blood to a heart that will beat no more.

For Winter came: the wind was his whip:
One choppy finger was on his lip:
He had torn the cataracts from the hills
And they clanked at his girdle like manacles;

His breath was a chain which without a sound
The earth, and the air, and the water bound;
He came, fiercely driven, in his chariot-throne   270
By the tenfold blasts of the Arctic zone.

Then the weeds which were forms of living death
Fled from the frost to the earth beneath.
Their decay and sudden flight from frost
Was but like the vanishing of a ghost!

And under the roots of the Sensitive Plant
The moles and the dormice died for want:
The birds dropped stiff from the frozen air
And were caught in the branches naked and bare.

First there came down a thawing rain   280
And its dull drops froze on the boughs again;
Then there steamed up a freezing dew
Which to the drops of the thaw-rain grew;

And a northern whirlwind, wandering about
Like a wolf that had smelt a dead child out,
Shook the boughs thus laden, and heavy, and stiff,
And snapped them off with his rigid griff.

When Winter had gone and Spring came back
The Sensitive Plant was a leafless wreck;
But the mandrakes, and toadstools, and docks, and
    darnels, 290
Rose like the dead from their ruined charnels.

CONCLUSION

Whether the Sensitive Plant, or that
Which within its boughs like a Spirit sat,
Ere its outward form had known decay,
Now felt this change, I cannot say.

Whether that Lady's gentle mind,
No longer with the form combined
Which scattered love, as stars do light,
Found sadness, where it left delight,

I dare not guess; but in this life 300
Of error, ignorance, and strife,
Where nothing is, but all things seem,
And we the shadows of the dream,

It is a modest creed, and yet
Pleasant if one considers it,
To own that death itself must be,
Like all the rest, a mockery.

That garden sweet, that lady fair,
And all sweet shapes and odours there,
In truth have never passed away: 310
'Tis we, 'tis ours, are changed; not they.

For love, and beauty, and delight,
There is no death nor change: their might
Exceeds our organs, which endure
No light, being themselves obscure.

PERCY BYSSHE SHELLEY.

XXVI. ARETHUSA

I

ARETHUSA arose
From her couch of snows
In the Acroceraunian mountains,—
From cloud and from crag,
With many a jag,
Shepherding her bright fountains.
She leapt down the rocks,
With her rainbow locks
Streaming among the streams;—
Her steps paved with green   10
The downward ravine
Which slopes to the western gleams;
And gliding and springing
She went, ever singing,

In murmurs as soft as sleep;
    The Earth seemed to love her,
    And Heaven smiled above her,
As she lingered towards the deep.

II

    Then Alpheus bold,
    On his glacier cold,   20
With his trident the mountains strook;
    And opened a chasm
    In the rocks—with the spasm
All Erymanthus shook.
    And the black south wind
    It unsealed behind
The urns of the silent snow,
    And earthquake and thunder
    Did rend in sunder
The bars of the springs below.   30
    The beard and the hair
    Of the River-god were
Seen through the torrent's sweep,
    As he followed the light
    Of the fleet nymph's flight
To the brink of the Dorian deep.

III

    " Oh, save me! Oh, guide me!
    And bid the deep hide me,
For he grasps me now by the hair! "
    The loud Ocean heard,   40
    To its blue depth stirred,

And divided at her prayer;
    And under the water
    The Earth's white daughter
Fled like a sunny beam;
    Behind her descended
    Her billows, unblended
With the brackish Dorian stream:—
    Like a gloomy stain
    On the emerald main   50
Alpheus rushed behind,—
    As an eagle pursuing
    A dove to its ruin
Down the streams of the cloudy wind.

IV

    Under the bowers
    Where the Ocean Powers
Sit on their pearlèd thrones;
    Through the coral woods
    Of the weltering floods,
Over heaps of unvalued stones;   60
    Through the dim beams
    Which amid the streams
Weave a network of coloured light;
    And under the caves,
    Where the shadowy waves
Are as green as the forest's night:—
    Outspeeding the shark,
    And the sword-fish dark,

60. *Unvalued.* Invaluable; very precious.

Under the Ocean's foam,
   And up through the rifts   70
   Of the mountain clifts
They passed to their Dorian home.

V

   And now from their fountains
   In Enna's mountains,
Down one vale where the morning basks,
   Like friends once parted
   Grown single-hearted,
They ply their watery tasks.
   At sunrise they leap
   From their cradles steep   80
In the cave of the shelving hill;
   At noontide they flow
   Through the woods below
And the meadows of asphodel:
   And at night they sleep
   In the rocking deep
Beneath the Ortygian shore;—
   Like spirits that lie
   In the azure sky
When they love but live no more.   90

PERCY BYSSHE SHELLEY.

71. *Clifts.* Cliffs.

XXVII. LUCY GRAY:

OR SOLITUDE

Written at Goslar in Germany. It was founded on a circumstance told me by my sister, of a little girl who, not far from Halifax in Yorkshire, was bewildered in a snowstorm. Her footsteps were traced by her parents to the middle of the lock of a canal, and no other vestige of her, backward or forward, could be traced. The body, however, was found in the canal.

OFT I had heard of Lucy Gray:
And, when I crossed the wild,
I chanced to see at break of day
The solitary child.

No mate, no comrade Lucy knew;
She dwelt on a wide moor.
—The sweetest thing that ever grew
Beside a human door!

You yet may spy the fawn at play,
The hare upon the green;   10
But the sweet face of Lucy Gray
Will never more be seen.

" To-night will be a stormy night—
You to the town must go;
And take a lantern, Child, to light
Your mother through the snow."

" That, Father! will I gladly do:
'Tis scarcely afternoon—
The minster-clock has just struck two,
And yonder is the moon! "   20

At this the Father raised his hook,
And snapped a faggot-band;
He plied his work;—and Lucy took
The lantern in her hand.

Not blither is the mountain roe:
With many a wanton stroke
Her feet disperse the powdery snow,
That rises up like smoke.

The storm came on before its time:
She wandered up and down;   30
And many a hill did Lucy climb:
But never reached the town.

The wretched parents all that night
Went shouting far and wide;
But there was neither sound nor sight
To serve them for a guide.

At day-break on a hill they stood
That overlooked the moor;
And thence they saw the bridge of wood,
A furlong from their door.   40

They wept—and, turning homeward, cried,
" In heaven we all shall meet ";
—When in the snow the mother spied
The print of Lucy's feet.

Then downwards from the steep hill's edge
They tracked the footmarks small;
And through the broken hawthorn hedge,
And by the long stone-wall;

And then an open field they crossed:
The marks were still the same;   50
They tracked them on, nor ever lost;
And to the bridge they came.

They followed from the snowy bank
Those footmarks, one by one,
Into the middle of the plank;
And further there were none!

—Yet some maintain that to this day
She is a living child;
That you may see sweet Lucy Gray
Upon the lonesome wild.   60

O'er rough and smooth she trips along,
And never looks behind;
And sings a solitary song
That whistles in the wind.

                    WILLIAM WORDSWORTH.

XXVIII. LAODAMIA

Written at Rydal Mount. The incident of the trees growing
and withering put the subject into my thoughts, and I wrote
with the hope of giving it a loftier tone than, so far as I know,
has been given to it by any of the Ancients who have treated
of it. It cost me more trouble than almost anything of equal
length I have ever written. [*Wordsworth's note.*]

" WITH sacrifice before the rising morn
Vows have I made by fruitless hope inspired;
And from the infernal Gods, 'mid shades forlorn
Of night, my slaughtered Lord have I required:
Celestial pity I again implore;—
Restore him to my sight—great Jove, restore! "

So speaking, and by fervent love endowed
With faith, the Suppliant heavenward lifts her hands;
While, like the sun emerging from a cloud,
Her countenance brightens—and her eye expands; 10
Her bosom heaves and spreads, her stature grows;
And she expects the issue in repose.

O terror! what hath she perceived?—O joy!
What doth she look on?—whom doth she behold?
Her Hero slain upon the beach of Troy?
His vital presence? his corporeal mould?
It is—if sense deceive her not—'tis He!
And a God leads him, wingèd Mercury!

E

Mild Hermes spake—and touched her with his wand
That calms all fear; " Such grace hath crowned thy
        prayer,   20
Laodamía! that at Jove's command
Thy Husband walks the paths of upper air:
He comes to tarry with thee three hours' space;
Accept the gift, behold him face to face! "

Forth sprang the impassioned Queen her Lord to clasp;
Again that consummation she essayed;
But unsubstantial Form eludes her grasp
As often as that eager grasp was made.
The Phantom parts—but parts to reunite,
And re-assumes his place before her sight.   30

" Protesiláus, lo! thy guide is gone!
Confirm, I pray, the vision with thy voice:
This is our palace,—yonder is thy throne:
Speak, and the floor thou tread'st on will rejoice.
Not to appal me have the gods bestowed
This precious boon; and blest a sad abode."

" Great Jove, Laodamía! doth not leave
His gifts imperfect:—Spectre though I be,
I am not sent to scare thee or deceive;
But in reward of thy fidelity.   40
And something also did my worth obtain;
For fearless virtue bringeth boundless gain.

" Thou knowest, the Delphic oracle foretold
That the first Greek who touched the Trojan strand

Should die; but me the threat could not withhold:
A generous cause a victim did demand;
And forth I leapt upon the sandy plain;
A self-devoted chief—by Hector slain."

" Supreme of Heroes—bravest, noblest, best!
Thy matchless courage I bewail no more,   50
Which then, when tens of thousands were deprest
By doubt, propelled thee to the fatal shore;
Thou found'st—and I forgive thee—here thou art—
A nobler counsellor than my poor heart.

" But thou, though capable of sternest deed,
Wert kind as resolute, and good as brave;
And he, whose power restores thee, hath decreed
Thou should'st elude the malice of the grave:
Redundant are thy locks, thy lips as fair
As when their breath enriched Thessalian air.   60

" No Spectre greets me,—no vain Shadow this;
Come, blooming Hero, place thee by my side!
Give, on this well-known couch, one nuptial kiss
To me, this day, a second time thy bride! "
Jove frowned in heaven: the conscious Parcæ threw
Upon those roseate lips a Stygian hue.

" This visage tells thee that my doom is past;
Nor should the change be mourned, even if the joys
Of sense were able to return as fast
And surely as they vanish. Earth destroys   70

65. *Parcæ.* Fates.

Those raptures duly—Erebus disdains:
Calm pleasures there abide—majestic pains.

" Be taught, O faithful Consort, to control
Rebellious passion; for the Gods approve
The depth, and not the tumult, of the soul;
A fervent, not ungovernable, love.
Thy transports moderate; and meekly mourn
When I depart,—for brief is my sojourn——"

" Ah, wherefore?—Did not Hercules by force
Wrest from the guardian Monster of the tomb   80
Alcestis, a reanimated corse,
Given back to dwell on earth in vernal bloom?
Medea's spells dispersed the weight of years,
And Æson stood a youth 'mid youthful peers.

" The Gods to us are merciful—and they
Yet further may relent; for mightier far
Than strength of nerve and sinew, or the sway
Of magic potent over sun and star,
Is love, though oft to agony distrest,
And though his favourite seat be feeble woman's
        breast.   90

" But if thou goest, I follow——" " Peace! " he said,—
She looked upon him and was calmed and cheered;
The ghastly colour from his lips had fled;
In his deportment, shape, and mien appeared

71. *Duly.* In due course (of time).

Elysian beauty, melancholy grace,
Brought from a pensive though a happy, place.

He spake of love, such love as Spirits feel
In worlds whose course is equable and pure;
No fears to beat away—no strife to heal—
The past unsighed for, and the future sure;   100
Spake of heroic acts in graver mood
Revived, with finer harmony pursued;

Of all that is most beauteous—imaged there
In happier beauty; more pellucid streams,
An ampler ether, a diviner air,
And fields invested with purpureal gleams;
Climes which the sun, who sheds the brightest day
Earth knows, is all unworthy to survey.

Yet there the Soul shall enter which hath earned
That privilege by virtue.—" Ill," said he,   110
" The end of man's existence I discerned,
Who from ignoble games and revelry
Could draw, when we had parted, vain delight,
While tears were thy best pastime, day and night;

" And while my youthful peers before my eyes
(Each hero following his peculiar bent)
Prepared themselves for glorious enterprise
By martial sports,—or, seated in the tent,
Chieftains and kings in council were detained;
What time the fleet at Aulis lay enchained.   120

" The wished-for wind was given:—I then revolved
The oracle, upon the silent sea;
And, if no worthier led the way, resolved
That, of a thousand vessels, mine should be
The foremost prow in pressing to the strand,—
Mine the first blood that tinged the Trojan sand.

" Yet bitter, oft-times bitter, was the pang
When of thy loss I thought, belovèd Wife!
On thee too fondly did my memory hang,
And on the joys we shared in mortal life,—   130
The paths which we had trod—these fountains, flowers,
My new-planned cities, and unfinished towers.

" But should suspense permit the Foe to cry,
' Behold they tremble!—haughty their array,
Yet of their number no one dares to die '?
In soul I swept the indignity away:
Old frailties then recurred:—but lofty thought,
In act embodied, my deliverance wrought.

" And Thou, though strong in love, art all too weak
In reason, in self-government too slow;   140
I counsel thee by fortitude to seek
Our blest re-union in the shades below.
The invisible world with thee hath sympathised;
Be thy affections raised and solemnised.

" Learn, by a mortal yearning, to ascend—
Seeking a higher object. Love was given,
Encouraged, sanctioned, chiefly for that end;
For this the passion to excess was driven—

The morn was wasted in the pathless grass,
And long and lonesome was the wild to pass; 30
But when the southern sun had warm'd the day,
A youth came posting o'er a crossing way;
His raiment decent, his complexion fair,
And soft in graceful ringlets wav'd his hair.
Then near approaching, " Father, hail! " he cried;
" And hail, my son," the reverend sire replied;
Words follow'd words, from question answer flow'd,
And talk of various kind deceiv'd the road;
Till each with other pleas'd, and loth to part,
While in their age they differ, join in heart: 40
Thus stands an aged elm in ivy bound,
Thus youthful ivy clasps an elm around.

Now sunk the sun; the closing hour of day
Came onward, mantled o'er with sober grey;
Nature in silence bid the world repose;
When near the road a stately palace rose:
There by the moon through ranks of trees they pass,
Whose verdure crown'd their sloping sides of
    grass.
It chanc'd the noble master of the dome
Still made his house the wandering stranger's home:
Yet still the kindness, from a thirst of praise, 51
Prov'd the vain flourish of expensive ease.
The pair arrive: the liveried servants wait;
Their lord receives them at the pompous gate.
The table groans with costly piles of food,
And all is more than hospitably good.

38. *Deceiv'd*. Beguiled.   49. *Dome*. House.
        50. *Still*. Always.

Then led to rest, the day's long toil they drown,
Deep sunk in sleep, and silk, and heaps of down.
   At length 'tis morn, and at the dawn of day,
Along the wide canals the zephyrs play;
Fresh o'er the gay parterres the breezes creep,   60
And shake the neighbouring wood to banish sleep.
Up rise the guests, obedient to the call:
An early banquet deck'd the splendid hall;
Rich luscious wine a golden goblet grac'd,
Which the kind master forc'd the guests to taste.
Then, pleas'd and thankful, from the porch they go;
And, but the landlord, none had cause of woe;
His cup was vanish'd; for in secret guise
The younger guest purloin'd the glittering prize.
   As one who spies a serpent in his way,   70
Glistening and basking in the summer ray,
Disorder'd stops to shun the danger near,
Then walks with faintness on, and looks with fear;
So seem'd the sire, when, far upon the road,
The shining spoil his wily partner show'd.
He stopp'd with silence, walk'd with trembling heart,
And much he wish'd, but durst not ask to part:
Murmuring he lifts his eyes, and thinks it hard,
That generous actions meet a base reward.
   While thus they pass, the sun his glory shrouds, 80
The changing skies hang out their sable clouds;
A sound in air presag'd approaching rain,
And beasts to covert scud across the plain.
Warn'd by the signs, the wandering pair retreat,
To seek for shelter at a neighbouring seat.

59. *Canals.* Ornamental waters.

'Twas built with turrets, on a rising ground,
And strong, and large, and unimprov'd around;
Its owner's temper, timorous and severe,
Unkind and griping, caus'd a desert there.

As near the miser's heavy doors they drew,   90
Fierce rising gusts with sudden fury blew;
The nimble lightning mix'd with showers began,
And o'er their heads loud rolling thunder ran.
Here long they knock, but knock or call in vain,
Driven by the wind, and batter'd by the rain.
At length some pity warm'd the master's breast,
('Twas then his threshold first receiv'd a guest,)
Slow creaking turns the door with jealous care,
And half he welcomes in the shivering pair;
One frugal faggot lights the naked walls,   100
And nature's fervour through their limbs recalls:
Bread of the coarsest sort, with eager wine,
Each hardly granted, serv'd them both to dine;
And when the tempest first appear'd to cease,
A ready warning bid them part in peace.
With still remark the pondering hermit view'd
In one so rich, a life so poor and rude;
And why should such, within himself he cried,
Lock the lost wealth a thousand want beside?
But what new marks of wonder soon took place 110
In every settling feature of his face,
When from his vest the young companion bore

102. *Eager.* Sour; French *aigre.*
106. *Still remark.* Silent observation.
111. *Settling.* Recovering from his surprise.
112. *Vest.* Clothes.

That cup, the generous landlord own'd before,
And paid profusely with the precious bowl
The stinted kindness of this churlish soul!

But now the clouds in airy tumult fly;
The sun emerging opes an azure sky;
A fresher green the smelling leaves display,
And, glittering as they tremble, cheer the day:
The weather courts them from the poor retreat,   120
And the glad master bolts the wary gate.

While hence they walk, the pilgrim's bosom wrought
With all the travail of uncertain thought;
His partner's acts without their cause appear,
'Twas there a vice, and seem'd a madness here:
Detesting that, and pitying this, he goes,
Lost and confounded with the various shows.

Now night's dim shades again involve the sky,
Again the wanderers want a place to lie,
Again they search, and find a lodging nigh: 130
The soil improv'd around, the mansion neat,
And neither poorly low, nor idly great:
It seem'd to speak its master's turn of mind,
Content, and not for praise, but virtue, kind.

Hither the walkers turn with weary feet,
Then bless the mansion, and the master greet:
Their greeting fair bestow'd, with modest guise,
The courteous master hears, and thus replies:

" Without a vain, without a grudging heart,
To Him who gives us all, I yield a part;   140
From Him you come, for Him accept it here,
A frank and sober, more than costly cheer."
He spoke, and bid the welcome table spread,

Then talk'd of virtue till the time of bed,
When the grave household round his hall repair,
Warn'd by a bell, and close the hours with prayer.
    At length the world, renew'd by calm repose,
Was strong for toil, the dappled morn arose.
Before the pilgrims part, the younger crept
Near the clos'd cradle where an infant slept,   150
And writh'd his neck: the landlord's little pride,
O strange return! grew black, and gasp'd, and died.
Horror of horrors! what! his only son!
How look'd our hermit when the fact was done?
Not hell, though hell's black jaws in sunder part,
And breathe blue fire, could more assault his heart.
    Confus'd and struck with silence at the deed,
He flies, but, trembling, fails to fly with speed,
His steps the youth pursues: the country lay
Perplex'd with roads, a servant show'd the way: 160
A river cross'd the path; the passage o'er
Was nice to find; the servant trod before:
Long arms of oaks an open bridge supplied,
And deep the waves beneath the bending glide.
The youth, who seem'd to watch a time to sin,
Approach'd the careless guide, and thrust him in;
Plunging he falls, and rising lifts his head,
Then flashing turns, and sinks among the dead.
    Wild, sparkling rage inflames the father's eyes,
He bursts the bands of fear, and madly cries,   170
" Detested wretch! "—but scarce his speech began,
When the strange partner seem'd no longer man:

154. *Fact.* Deed.   162. *Nice.* Difficult.
166. *Careless.* Unsuspecting.

His youthful face grew more serenely sweet;
His robe turn'd white, and flow'd upon his feet;
Fair rounds of radiant points invest his hair;
Celestial odours breathe through purpled air;
And wings, whose colours glitter'd on the day,
Wide at his back their gradual plumes display.
The form ethereal bursts upon his sight,
And moves in all the majesty of light.   180

    Though loud at first the pilgrim's passion grew,
Sudden he gaz'd, and wist not what to do;
Surprise in secret chains his words suspends,
And in a calm his settling temper ends.
But silence here the beauteous angel broke,
The voice of music ravish'd as he spoke.

    " Thy prayer, thy praise, thy life to vice unknown,
In sweet memorial rise before the throne:
These charms, success in our bright region find,
And force an angel down, to calm thy mind;   190
For this commission'd, I forsook the sky,
Nay, cease to kneel—thy fellow-servant I.

    " Then know the truth of government divine,
And let these scruples be no longer thine.

    " The Maker justly claims that world He made,
In this the right of Providence is laid;
Its sacred majesty through all depends
On using second means to work His ends:
'Tis thus, withdrawn in state from human eye,
The Power exerts His attributes on high,   200
Your actions uses, nor controls your will,

175. *Invest.* Clothe.
198. *Second.* God Himself being the First Cause of all.

And bids the doubting sons of men be still.
  "What strange events can strike with more
    surprise,
Than those which lately struck thy wondering eyes?
Yet taught by these, confess th' Almighty just,
And where you can't unriddle, learn to trust!
  "The great, vain man, who far'd on costly food,
Whose life was too luxurious to be good;
Who made his ivory stands with goblets shine,
And forc'd his guests to morning draughts of wine,
Has, with the cup, the graceless custom lost,   211
And still he welcomes, but with less of cost.
  "The mean, suspicious wretch, whose bolted door
Ne'er mov'd in duty to the wandering poor;
With him I left the cup, to teach his mind
That heaven can bless, if mortals will be kind.
Conscious of wanting worth, he views the bowl,
And feels compassion touch his grateful soul.
Thus artists melt the sullen ore of lead,
With heaping coals of fire upon its head;   220
In the kind warmth the metal learns to glow,
And loose from dross, the silver runs below.
  "Long had our pious friend in virtue trod,
But now the child half-wean'd his heart from God;
Child of his age, for him he liv'd in pain,
And measur'd back his steps to earth again.
To what excesses had this dotage run!
But God, to save the father, took the son.

       219. *Artists.* Artificers: here means plumbers.
       222. *Silver.* The pure silvery metal.
       227. *Had.* Would have.

To all but thee, in fits he seem'd to go,
And 'twas my ministry to deal the blow.   230
The poor fond parent, humbled in the dust,
Now owns in tears the punishment was just.

   " But how had all his fortune felt a wrack,
Had that false servant sped in safety back!
This night his treasur'd heaps he meant to steal,
And what a fund of charity would fail!

   " Thus Heaven instructs thy mind: this trial o'er,
Depart in peace, resign'd, and sin no more."

   On sounding pinions here the youth withdrew,
The sage stood wondering as the seraph flew.   240
Thus look'd Elisha, when, to mount on high,
His master took the chariot of the sky;
The fiery pomp ascending left the view;
The prophet gaz'd, and wish'd to follow too.

   The bending hermit here a prayer begun,
" Lord! as in heaven, on earth thy will be done! "
Then gladly turning, sought his ancient place,
And pass'd a life of piety and peace.

                                        THOMAS PARNELL.

   229. *In fits.* Everyone else thought the child had died of
a fit.

Revolving in his altered soul
The various turns of chance below;
And, now and then, a sigh he stole,
    And tears began to flow.

CHORUS

Revolving in his altered soul
The various turns of chance below;   90
And, now and then, a sigh he stole,
    And tears began to flow.

V

The mighty master smiled to see
That love was in the next degree;
'Twas but a kindred sound to move,
For pity melts the mind to love.
    Softly sweet, in Lydian measures,
    Soon he soothed his soul to pleasures.
    War, he sung, is toil and trouble;
    Honour but an empty bubble;   100
    Never ending, still beginning,
        Fighting still, and still destroying:
    If the world be worth thy winning,
        Think, O think it worth enjoying:
    Lovely Thais sits beside thee,
    Take the good the gods provide thee.
The many rend the skies with loud applause;
So Love was crowned, but Music won the cause.
The prince, unable to conceal his pain,
        Gazed on the fair   110
        Who caused his care,

And sighed and looked, sighed and looked,
    Sighed and looked, and sighed again;
At length, with love and wine at once oppressed,
The vanquished victor sunk upon her breast.

CHORUS

The prince, unable to conceal his pain,
        Gazed on the fair
        Who caused his care,
    And sighed and looked, sighed and looked,
        Sighed and looked, and sighed again;   120
At length, with love and wine at once oppressed,
The vanquished victor sunk upon her breast.

VI

Now strike the golden lyre again;
A louder yet, and yet a louder strain.
Break his bands of sleep asunder,
And rouse him, like a rattling peal of thunder.
        Hark, hark, the horrid sound
        Has raised up his head;
        As awaked from the dead,
    And amazed, he stared around,   130
Revenge, revenge, Timotheus cries,
        See the Furies arise;

114. *At once*. At the same time.
131. *Timotheus*. A musician of Bœotia, a favourite of Alexander the Great; not the great musician, Timotheus, who died
before Alexander was born; unless Dryden has confused the
two.

See the snakes that they rear,
How they hiss in their hair,
And the sparkles that flash from their eyes!
Behold a ghastly band,
Each a torch in his hand!
Those are Grecian ghosts, that in battle were slain,
And unburied remain
Inglorious on the plain: 140
Give the vengeance due
To the valiant crew.
Behold how they toss their torches on high,
How they point to the Persian abodes,
And glittering temples of their hostile gods.
The princes applaud with a furious joy;
And the king seized a flambeau with zeal to destroy;
Thais led the way,
To light him to his prey,
And, like another Helen, fired another Troy.   150

CHORUS

And the king seized a flambeau with zeal to destroy;
Thais led the way,
To light him to his prey,
And, like another Helen, fired another Troy.

VII

Thus long ago,
Ere heaving bellows learned to blow,
While organs yet were mute,
Timotheus, to his breathing flute
And sounding lyre,

Could swell the soul to rage, or kindle soft desire. 160
    At last divine Cecilia came,
    Inventress of the vocal frame;
The sweet enthusiast, from her sacred store,
    Enlarged the former narrow bounds,
    And added length to solemn sounds,
With nature's mother-wit, and arts unknown before.
    Let old Timotheus yield the prize,
      Or both divide the crown:
    He raised a mortal to the skies;
      She drew an angel down. 170

GRAND CHORUS

    At last divine Cecilia came,
    Inventress of the vocal frame;
The sweet enthusiast, from her sacred store,
    Enlarged the former narrow bounds,
    And added length to solemn sounds,
With Nature's mother-wit, and arts unknown before.
    Let old Timotheus yield the prize,
      Or both divide the crown:
    He raised a mortal to the skies;
      She drew an angel down. 180

JOHN DRYDEN.

XXXI. ON THE DEATH OF A FAVOURITE CAT

DROWNED IN A TUB OF GOLD FISHES

On a favourite cat called Selima, that fell into a china tub with gold fishes in it, and was drowned. Walpole, after the death of Gray, placed the china vase on a pedestal at Strawberry Hill, with a few lines of the Ode for its inscription.

'TWAS on a lofty vase's side,
Where China's gayest art had dy'd
   The azure flowers, that blow;
Demurest of the tabby kind,
The pensive Selima, reclin'd,
   Gaz'd on the lake below.

Her conscious tail her joy declar'd;
The fair round face, the snowy beard,
   The velvet of her paws,
Her coat, that with the tortoise vies,   10
Her ears of jet, and emerald eyes,
   She saw; and purr'd applause.

Still had she gaz'd; but 'midst the tide
Two angel forms were seen to glide,
   The Genii of the stream:
Their scaly armour's Tyrian hue
Through richest purple to the view
   Betray'd a golden gleam.

3. *Blow.* Bloom.

The hapless nymph with wonder saw:
A whisker first, and then a claw,   20
  With many an ardent wish,
She stretch'd, in vain, to reach the prize.
What female heart can gold despise?
  What cat's averse to fish?

Presumptuous maid! with looks intent
Again she stretch'd, again she bent,
  Nor knew the gulf between.
(Malignant Fate sat by, and smil'd)
The slipp'ry verge her feet beguil'd,
  She tumbled headlong in.   30

Eight times emerging from the flood
She mew'd to ev'ry wat'ry God,
  Some speedy aid to send.
Nor Dolphin came, nor Nereid stirr'd:
Nor cruel Tom, nor Susan heard.
  A fav'rite has no friend!

From hence, ye beauties, undeceiv'd,
Know, one false step is ne'er retriev'd,
  And be with caution bold.
Not all that tempts your wand'ring eyes   40
And heedless hearts is lawful prize,
  Nor all that glisters, gold.

                              THOMAS GRAY.

XXXII. THE NEEDLESS ALARM

A TALE

THERE is a field through which I often pass,
Thick overspread with moss and silky grass,
Adjoining close to Kilwick's echoing wood,
Where oft the bitch-fox hides her hapless brood,
Reserved to solace many a neighbouring squire,
That he may follow them through brake and brier,
Contusion hazarding of neck or spine,
Which rural gentlemen call sport divine.
A narrow brook, by rushy banks concealed,
Runs in a bottom, and divides the field;   10
Oaks intersperse it, that had once a head,
But now wear crests of oven-wood instead;
And where the land slopes to its watery bourn
Wide yawns a gulf beside a ragged thorn;
Bricks line the sides, but shivered long ago,
And horrid brambles intertwine below;
A hollow scooped, I judge, in ancient time,
For baking earth, or burning rock to lime.
   Not yet the hawthorn bore her berries red,
With which the fieldfare, wintry guest, is fed;   20
Nor Autumn yet had brushed from every spray,
With her chill hand, the mellow leaves away;
But corn was housed, and beans were in the stack;
Now therefore issued forth the spotted pack,
With tails high mounted, ears hung low, and throats
With a whole gamut filled of heavenly notes,

For which, alas! my destiny severe,
Though ears she gave me two, gave me no ear.
  The sun, accomplishing his early march,
His lamp now planted on heaven's topmost arch,   30
When, exercise and air my only aim,
And heedless whither, to that field I came,
Ere yet with ruthless joy the happy hound
Told hill and dale that Reynard's track was found,
Or with the high-raised horn's melodious clang
All Kilwick and all Dinglederry rang.
  Sheep grazed the field; some with soft bosom pressed
The herb as soft, while nibbling strayed the rest;
Nor noise was heard but of the hasty brook,
Struggling, detained in many a petty nook.   40
  All seemed so peaceful, that from them conveyed,
To me their peace by kind contagion spread.
  But when the huntsman, with distended cheek,
'Gan make his instrument of music speak,
And from within the wood that crash was heard,
Though not a hound from whom it burst appeared,
The sheep recumbent and the sheep that grazed,
All huddling into phalanx, stood and gazed,
Admiring, terrified, the novel strain,
Then coursed the field around, and coursed it round
    again;   50
But recollecting, with a sudden thought
That flight in circles urged advanced them nought,
They gathered close around the old pit's brink,
And thought again—but knew not what to think.

    36. *Kilwick* and *Dinglederry*. Two woods belonging to John
Throckmorton, Esq.

The man to solitude accustomed long
Perceives in every thing that lives a tongue;
Not animals alone, but shrubs and trees
Have speech for him, and understood with ease;
After long drought, when rains abundant fall,
He hears the herbs and flowers rejoicing all;   60
Knows what the freshness of their hue implies,
How glad they catch the largess of the skies;
But, with precision nicer still, the mind
He scans of every locomotive kind;
Birds of all feather, beasts of every name,
That serve mankind or shun them, wild or tame;
The looks and gestures of their griefs and fears
Have all articulation in his ears;
He spells them true by intuition's light,
And needs no glossary to set him right.   70
   This truth premised was needful as a text,
To win due credence to what follows next.
   Awhile they mused; surveying every face,
Thou hadst supposed them of superior race;
Their periwigs of wool and fears combined
Stamped on each countenance such marks of mind,
That sage they seemed, as lawyers o'er a doubt,
Which, puzzling long, at last they puzzle out;
Or academic tutors, teaching youths,
Sure ne'er to want them, mathematic truths;   80
When thus a mutton statelier than the rest,
A Ram, the ewes and wethers sad addressed:
   " Friends! we have lived too long. I never heard
Sounds such as these, so worthy to be feared.
Could I believe, that winds for ages pent

In earth's dark womb have found at last a vent,
And from their prison-house below arise,
With all these hideous howlings to the skies,
I could be much composed, nor should appear,
For such a cause, to feel the slightest fear.   90
Yourselves have seen, what time the thunders rolled
All night, me resting quiet in the fold.
Or heard we that tremendous bray alone,
I could expound the melancholy tone;
Should deem it by our old companion made,
The Ass; for he, we know, has lately strayed,
And being lost, perhaps, and wandering wide,
Might be supposed to clamour for a guide.
But ah! those dreadful yells what soul can hear
That owns a carcass, and not quake for fear?   100
Demons produce them doubtless, brazen-clawed,
And fanged with brass, the demons are abroad;
I hold it therefore wisest and most fit
That, life to save, we leap into the pit."

    Him answered then his loving mate and true,
But more discreet than he, a Cambrian Ewe:
    " How! leap into the pit our life to save?
To save our life leap all into the grave?
For can we find it less? Contemplate first
The depth how awful! falling there, we burst: 110
Or should the brambles interposed our fall
In part abate, that happiness were small;
For with a race like theirs no chance I see
Of peace or ease to creatures clad as we.
Meantime, noise kills not. Be it Dapple's bray,
Or be it not, or be it whose it may,

And rush those other sounds, that seem by tongues
Of demons uttered, from whatever lungs,
Sounds are but sounds, and, till the cause appear,
We have at least commodious standing here.   120
Come fiend, come fury, giant, monster, blast
From earth or hell, we can but plunge at last."
  While thus she spake, I fainter heard the peals,
For Reynard close attended at his heels
By panting dog, tired man, and spattered horse,
Through mere good fortune took a different course.
The flock grew calm again, and I, the road
Following, that led me to my own abode,
Much wondered that the silly sheep had found
Such cause of terror in an empty sound,   130
So sweet to huntsman, gentleman, and hound.

MORAL

Beware of desperate steps. The darkest day,
Live till to-morrow, will have passed away.
                              WILLIAM COWPER.

XXXIII. THE COLUBRIAD

CLOSE by the threshold of a door nailed fast
Three kittens sat; each kitten looked aghast.
I, passing swift and inattentive by,
At the three kittens cast a careless eye;
Not much concerned to know what they did there;
Not deeming kittens worth a poet's care.

But presently a loud and furious hiss
Caused me to stop, and to exclaim, " What's this? "
When lo! upon the threshold met my view,
With head erect, and eyes of fiery hue,   10
A viper, long as Count de Grasse's queue.
Forth from his head his forkèd tongue he throws,
Darting it full against a kitten's nose;
Who having never seen, in field or house,
The like, sat still and silent as a mouse;
Only projecting, with attention due,
Her whiskered face, she asked him, " Who are you? "
On to the hall went I, with pace not slow,
But swift as lightning, for a long Dutch hoe:
With which well armed I hastened to the spot,   20
To find the viper, but I found him not.
And turning up the leaves and shrubs around,
Found only that he was not to be found.
But still the kittens, sitting as before,
Sat watching close the bottom of the door.
" I hope," said I, " the villain I would kill
Has slipped between the door and the door-sill;
And if I make despatch, and follow hard,
No doubt but I shall find him in the yard ":
For long ere now it should have been rehearsed,   30
'Twas in the garden that I found him first.
E'en there I found him, there the full-grown cat
His head, with velvet paw, did gently pat;
As curious as the kittens erst had been
To learn what this phenomenon might mean.
Filled with heroic ardour at the sight,
And fearing every moment he would bite,

And rob our household of our only cat
That was of age to combat with a rat,
With outstretched hoe I slew him at the door, 40
And taught him NEVER TO COME THERE NO MORE.

WILLIAM COWPER.

XXXIV. ON THE DEATH OF
MRS. THROCKMORTON'S BULLFINCH

YE Nymphs, if e'er your eyes were red
With tears o'er hapless favourites shed,
  Oh share Maria's grief!
Her favourite, even in his cage
(What will not hunger's cruel rage?)
  Assassined by a thief.

Where Rhenus strays his vines among
The egg was laid from which he sprung;
  And though by nature mute,
Or only with a whistle blessed, 10
Well-taught, he all the sounds expressed
  Of flageolet or flute.

The honours of his ebon poll
Were brighter than the sleekest mole,
  His bosom of the hue
With which Aurora decks the skies,
When piping winds shall soon arise
  To sweep away the dew.

7. *Rhenus.* Rhine.

Above, below, in all the house,
Dire foe alike of bird and mouse,   20
   No cat had leave to dwell;
And Bully's cage supported stood
On props of smoothest-shaven wood,
   Large-built and latticed well.

Well latticed—but the grate, alas!
Not rough with wire of steel or brass,
   For Bully's plumage sake,
But smooth with wands from Ouse's side,
With which, when neatly peeled and dried,
   The swains their baskets make.   30

Night veiled the pole; all seemed secure;
When, led by instinct sharp and sure,
   Subsistence to provide,
A beast forth sallied on the scout,
Long-backed, long-tailed, with whiskered
     snout,
   And badger-coloured hide.

He, entering at the study door,
Its ample area 'gan explore;
   And something in the wind
Conjectured, sniffing round and round,   40
Better than all the books he found,
   Food chiefly for the mind.

31. *Pole.* Sky.

Just then, by adverse fate impressed,
A dream disturbed poor Bully's rest;
　　In sleep he seemed to view
A rat fast clinging to the cage,
And screaming at the sad presage,
　　Awoke and found it true.

For, aided both by ear and scent,
Right to his mark the monster went,—   50
　　Ah, Muse! forbear to speak
Minute the horrors that ensued;
His teeth were strong, the cage was wood,—
　　He left poor Bully's beak.

Oh, had he made that too his prey!
That beak, whence issued many a lay
　　Of such mellifluous tone,
Might have repaid him well, I wote,
For silencing so sweet a throat,
　　Fast stuck within his own.   60

Maria weeps,—the Muses mourn;—
So, when by Bacchanalians torn,
　　On Thracian Hebrus' side
The tree-enchanter Orpheus fell,
His head alone remained to tell
　　The cruel death he died.

WILLIAM COWPER.

XXXV. THE HAUNCH OF VENISON

A Poetical Epistle to Lord Clare

THANKS, my Lord, for your venison, for finer or fatter
Never rang'd in a forest, or smok'd in a platter;
The haunch was a picture for painters to study,
The fat was so white, and the lean was so ruddy.
Though my stomach was sharp, I could scarce help regretting
To spoil such a delicate picture by eating;
I had thoughts, in my chambers to place it in view,
To be shown to my friends as a piece of *virtù*;
As in some Irish houses, where things are so so,
One gammon of bacon hangs up for a show: 10
But for eating a rasher of what they take pride in,
They'd as soon think of eating the pan it is fried in.
But hold—let me pause—Don't I hear you pronounce
This tale of the bacon a damnable bounce?
Well, suppose it a bounce—sure a poet may try,
By a bounce now and then, to get courage to fly.
But, my lord, it's no bounce: I protest in my turn,
It's a truth—and your Lordship may ask Mr. Byrne.
To go on with my tale—as I gaz'd on the haunch,
I thought of a friend that was trusty and staunch;   20
So I cut it, and sent in to Reynolds undress'd,
To paint it, or eat it, just as he lik'd best.

8. *Virtù.* A curio, antique or other product of Fine Art.
14. *Bounce.* Impudent lie.
18. *Mr. Byrne.* Lord Clare's nephew.

Of the neck and the breast I had next to dispose;
'Twas a neck and a breast—that might rival Monroe's:—
But in parting with these I was puzzled again,
With the how, and the who, and the where, and the when.

There's Howard, and Coley, and H——rth, and Hiff,
I think they love venison—I know they love beef;
There's my countryman Higgins—Oh! let him alone,
For making a blunder, or picking a bone.   30
But hang it—to poets who seldom can eat,
Your very good mutton's a very good treat;
Such dainties to them, their health it might hurt,
It's like sending them ruffles, when wanting a shirt.
While this I debated, in reverie centred,
An acquaintance, a friend as he call'd himself, enter'd;
An under-bred, fine-spoken fellow was he,
And he smil'd as he look'd at the venison and me.
" What have we got here?—Why this is good eating!
Your own, I suppose—or is it in waiting? "   40
" Why, whose should it be? " cried I with a flounce,
" I get these things often; "—but that was a bounce:
" Some lords, my acquaintance, that settle the nation,
Are pleas'd to be kind—but I hate ostentation."

" If that be the case, then," cried he, very gay,
" I'm glad I have taken this house in my way.
To-morrow you take a poor dinner with me;
No words—I insist on't—precisely at three:

24. *Monroe.* Dorothy Monroe, a celebrated beauty.
27. *Hiff.* Paul Hiffernan, M.D., a Grub Street writer.

We'll have Johnson, and Burke; all the wits will be there;
My acquaintance is slight, or I'd ask my Lord Clare.   50
And now that I think on't, as I am a sinner!
We wanted this venison to make out the dinner.
What say you—a pasty? it shall, and it must,
And my wife, little Kitty, is famous for crust.
Here, porter!—this venison with me to Mile-end;
No stirring—I beg—my dear friend—my dear friend!"
Thus snatching his hat, he brush'd off like the wind,
And the porter and eatables followed behind.

Left alone to reflect, having emptied my shelf,
" And nobody with me at sea but myself ";   60
Though I could not help thinking my gentleman hasty,
Yet Johnson, and Burke, and a good venison pasty,
Were things that I never dislik'd in my life,
Though clogged with a coxcomb, and Kitty his wife.
So next day, in due splendour to make my approach,
I drove to his door in my own hackney-coach.

When come to the place where we all were to dine,
(A chair-lumber'd closet just twelve feet by nine:)
My friend bade me welcome, but struck me quite dumb,
With tidings that Johnson and Burke would not come;   70
" For I knew it," he cried, " both eternally fail,
The one with his speeches, and t'other with Thrale;
But no matter, I warrant we'll make up the party
With two full as clever, and ten times as hearty.

72. *Thrale.* Mrs. Thrale, wife of the Southwark brewer, Johnson's
close friend from 1765.

The one is a Scotchman, the other a Jew,
They're both of them merry and authors like you;
The one writes the *Snarler*, the other the *Scourge*;
Some think he writes *Cinna*—he owns to *Panurge*."
While thus he describ'd them by trade and by name,
They enter'd, and dinner was serv'd as they came.   80

At the top a fried liver and bacon were seen,
At the bottom was tripe in a swinging tureen;
At the sides there was spinach and pudding made hot;
In the middle a place where the pasty—was not.
Now, my Lord, as for tripe, it's my utter aversion,
And your bacon I hate like a Turk or a Persian;
So there I sat stuck, like a horse in a pound,
While the bacon and liver went merrily round.
But what vex'd me most was that d——'d Scottish rogue,
With his long-winded speeches, his smiles and his brogue; 90
And, " Madam," quoth he, " may this bit be my poison,
A prettier dinner I never set eyes on;
Pray a slice of your liver, though may I be curs'd,
But I've eat of your tripe till I'm ready to burst."

" The tripe," quoth the Jew, with his chocolate cheek,
" I could dine on this tripe seven days in the week:
I like these here dinners so pretty and small;
But your friend there, the Doctor, eats nothing at all."
" O—Oh!" quoth my friend, " he'll come on in a trice,
He's keeping a corner for something that's nice: 100

79. *Cinna . . . Panurge.* These were *noms de guerre* of Dr. J. Scott,
Lord Sandwich's chaplain, an active supporter of the Government.

There's a pasty "—" A pasty!" repeated the Jew,
" I don't care if I keep a corner for't too."
" What the de'il, mon, a pasty!" re-echoed the Scot,
" Though splitting, I'll still keep a corner for thot."
" We'll all keep a corner," the lady cried out;
" We'll all keep a corner," was echoed about.
While thus we resolv'd, and the pasty delay'd,
With looks that quite petrified, enter'd the maid;
A visage so sad, and so pale with affright,
Wak'd Priam in drawing his curtains by night.   110
But we quickly found out, for who could mistake her?
That she came with some terrible news from the baker:
And so it fell out, for that negligent sloven
Had shut out the pasty on shutting his oven.
Sad Philomel thus—but let similes drop—
And now that I think on't, the story may stop.
To be plain, my good Lord, it's but labour misplaced
To send such good verses to one of your taste;
You've got an odd something—a kind of discerning—
A relish—a taste—sicken'd over by learning;   120
At least it's your temper, as very well known,
That you think very slightly of all that's your own:
So, perhaps, in your habits of thinking amiss,
You may make a mistake, and think slightly of this.

OLIVER GOLDSMITH.

XXXVI. ELEGY ON THE DEATH OF
A MAD DOG

Good people all, of every sort,
   Give ear unto my song;
And if you find it wond'rous short,
   It cannot hold you long.

In Islington there was a man,
   Of whom the world might say,
That still a godly race he ran,
   Whene'er he went to pray.

A kind and gentle heart he had,
   To comfort friends and foes;   10
The naked every day he clad,
   When he put on his clothes.

And in that town a dog was found,
   As many dogs there be,
Both mongrel, puppy, whelp, and hound,
   And curs of low degree.

This dog and man at first were friends;
   But when a pique began,
The dog, to gain some private ends,
   Went mad and bit the man.   20

Around from all the neighbouring streets
   The wond'ring neighbours ran,
And swore the dog had lost his wits,
   To bite so good a man.

The wound it seem'd both sore and sad
   To every Christian eye;
And while they swore the dog was mad,
   They swore the man would die.

But soon a wonder came to light,
   That show'd the rogues they lied: 30
The man recover'd of the bite,
   The dog it was that died.

                       OLIVER GOLDSMITH.

XXXVII. LLYN-Y-DREIDDIAD-VRAWD

The Pool of the Diving Friar

Gwenwynwyn withdrew from the feasts of his hall;
He slept very little, he prayed not at all;
He pondered, and wandered, and studied alone;
And sought, night and day, the philosopher's stone.

He found it at length, and he made its first proof
By turning to gold all the lead of his roof:
Then he bought some magnanimous heroes, all fire,
Who lived but to smite and be smitten for hire.

With these, on the plains like a torrent he broke;
He filled the whole country with flame and with smoke;   10
He killed all the swine, and he broached all the wine;
He drove off the sheep, and the beeves, and the kine;

He took castles and towns; he cut short limbs and lives;
He made orphans and widows of children and wives:
This course many years he triumphantly ran,
And did mischief enough to be called a great man.

When, at last, he had gained all for which he had striven,
He bethought him of buying a passport to heaven;
Good and great as he was, yet he did not well know
How soon, or which way, his great spirit might go.   20

He sought the grey friars, who, beside a wild stream,
Refected their frames on a primitive scheme;
The gravest and wisest Gwenwynwyn found out,
All lonely and ghostly, and angling for trout.

Below the white dash of a mighty cascade,
Where a pool of the stream a deep resting-place made,
And rock-rooted oaks stretched their branches on high,
The friar stood musing, and throwing his fly.

To him said Gwenwynwyn, " Hold, father, here's store,
For the good of the church, and the good of the poor ";   30
Then he gave him the stone; but, ere more he could speak,
Wrath came on the friar, so holy and meek.

He had stretched forth his hand to receive the red gold,
And he thought himself mocked by Gwenwynwyn the Bold;
And in scorn of the gift, and in rage at the giver,
He jerked it immediately into the river.

Gwenwynwyn, aghast, not a syllable spake;
The philosopher's stone made a duck and a drake:
Two systems of circles a moment were seen,
And the stream smoothed them off, as they never had been.   40

Gwenwynwyn regained, and uplifted, his voice:
"Oh friar, grey friar, full rash was thy choice;
The stone, the good stone, which away thou hast thrown,
Was the stone of all stones, the philosopher's stone!"

The friar looked pale, when his error he knew;
The friar looked red, and the friar looked blue;
And heels over head, from the point of a rock,
He plunged, without stopping to pull off his frock.

He dived very deep, but he dived all in vain;
The prize he had slighted he found not again: 50
Many times did the friar his diving renew,
And deeper and deeper the river still grew.

Gwenwynwyn gazed long, of his senses in doubt,
To see the grey friar a diver so stout:
Then sadly and slowly his castle he sought,
And left the friar diving, like dabchick distraught.

Gwenwynwyn fell sick with alarm and despite,
Died, and went to the devil, the very same night:
The magnanimous heroes he held in his pay
Sacked his castle, and marched with the plunder away.   60

No knell on the silence of midnight was rolled,
For the flight of the soul of Gwenwynwyn the Bold:
The brethren, unfee'd, let the mighty ghost pass
Without praying a prayer, or intoning a mass.

The friar haunted ever beside the dark stream:
The philosopher's stone was his thought and his dream;
And day after day, ever head under heels,
He dived all the time he could spare from his meals.

He dived, and he dived, to the end of his days,
As the peasants oft witnessed with fear and amaze: 70
The mad friar's diving-place long was their theme,
And no plummet can fathom that pool of the stream.

And still, when light clouds on the midnight winds ride,
If by moonlight you stray on the lone river-side,
The ghost of the friar may be seen diving there,
With head in the water and heels in the air.

                                    THOMAS LOVE PEACOCK.

XXXVIII. THE BATTLE OF LIMERICK

            YE Genii of the nation,
            Who look with veneration,
And Ireland's desolation onsaysingly deplore;
            Ye sons of General Jackson,
            Who thrample on the Saxon,
Attend to the thransaction upon Shannon shore.

            When William, Duke of Schumbug,
            A tyrant and a humbug,
With cannon and with thunder on our city bore,
            Our fortitude and valliance,   10
            Insthructed his battalions
To rispict the gallant Irish upon Shannon shore.

            Since that capitulation,
            No city in this nation
So grand a reputation could boast before,

As Limerick prodigious,
That stands with quays and bridges,
And the ships up to the windies of the Shannon shore.

A chief of ancient line,
'Tis William Smith O'Brine,   20
Reprisints this darling Limerick, this ten years or more:
O the Saxons can't endure
To see him on the flure,
And thrimble at the Cicero from Shannon shore.

This valliant son of Mars
Had been to visit Par's,
That land of Revolution, that grows the tricolor;
And to welcome his return
From pilgrimages furren,
We invited him to tay on the Shannon shore.   30

Then we summoned to our board
Young Meagher of the Sword;
'Tis he will sheathe that battle-axe in Saxon gore:
And Mitchil of Belfast
We bade to our repast,
To dthrink a dish of coffee on the Shannon shore.

Convaniently to hould
These patriots so bould,
We tuck the opportunity of Tim Doolan's store;
And with ornamints and banners   40
(As becomes gintale good manners)
We made the loveliest tay-room upon Shannon shore.

'Twould binifit your sowls,
To see the butthered rowls,
The sugar-tongs and sangwidges and craim galyore,
And the muffins and the crumpets,
And the band of harps and thrumpets,
To celebrate the sworry upon Shannon shore.

Sure the Imperor of Bohay
Would be proud to dthrink the tay   50
That Misthress Biddy Rooney for O'Brine did pour;
And, since the days of Strongbow,
There never was such Congo—
Mitchil dthrank six quarts of it—by Shannon shore.

But Clarndon and Corry
Connellan beheld this sworry
With rage and imulation in their black hearts' core;
They hired a gang of ruffins
To interrupt the muffins
And the fragrance of the Congo on the Shannon shore.   60

When full of tay and cake,
O'Brine began to spake;
But juice a one could hear him, for a sudden roar
Of a ragamuffin rout
Began to yell and shout,
And frighten the propriety of Shannon shore.

As Smith O'Brine harangued,
They batthered and they banged:
Tim Doolan's doors and windies down they tore;

They smashed the lovely windies   70
(Hung with muslin from the Indies),
Purshuing of their shindies upon Shannon shore.

With throwing of brickbats,
Drowned puppies and dead rats,
These ruffin democrats themselves did lower;
Tin kettles, rotten eggs,
Cabbage-stalks, and wooden legs,
They flung among the patriots of Shannon shore.

Oh the girls began to scrame
And upset the milk and crame;   80
And the honourable gintlemin, they cursed and swore:
And Mitchil of Belfast,
'Twas he that looked aghast,
When they roasted him in effigy by Shannon shore.

Oh the lovely tay was spilt
On that day of Ireland's guilt;
Says Jack Mitchil, "I am kilt! Boys, where's the back door?
'Tis a national disgrace;
Let me go and veil me face";
And he boulted with quick pace from the Shannon shore. 90

"Cut down the bloody horde!"
Says Meagher of the Sword,
This conduct would disgrace any blackamore";
But the best use Tommy made
Of his famous battle blade
Was to cut his own stick from the Shannon shore.

Immortal Smith O'Brine
Was raging like a line;
'Twould have done your sowl good to have heard him roar;
In his glory he arose,   100
And he rush'd upon his foes,
But they hit him on the nose by the Shannon shore.

Then the Futt and the Dthragoons
In squadthrons and platoons,
With their music playing chunes, down upon us bore:
And they beat the rattatoo,
But the Peelers came in view,
And ended the shaloo on the Shannon shore.

W. M. THACKERAY.

XXXIX. FAITHLESS SALLY BROWN

AN OLD BALLAD

YOUNG Ben he was a nice young man,
   A carpenter by trade;
And he fell in love with Sally Brown,
   That was a lady's maid.

But as they fetched a walk one day,
   They met a press-gang crew;
And Sally she did faint away,
   Whilst Ben he was brought to.

The Boatswain swore with wicked words,
   Enough to shock a saint,   10
That though she did seem in a fit,
   'Twas nothing but a feint.

" Come, girl," said he, " hold up your head,
   He'll be as good as me;
For when your swain is in our boat,
   A boatswain he will be."

So when they'd made their game of her,
   And taken off her elf,
She roused, and found she only was
   A coming to herself.

" And is he gone, and is he gone? "
   She cried, and wept outright:
" Then I will to the water side,
   And see him out of sight."

A waterman came up to her,
   " Now, young woman," said he,
" If you weep on so, you will make
   Eye-water in the sea."

" Alas! they've taken my beau Ben
   To sail with old Benbow ";   30
And her woe began to run afresh,
   As if she'd said Gee woe!

Says he, " They've only taken him
   To the Tender ship, you see ";
" The Tender ship," cried Sally Brown,
   " What a hard-ship that must be!

Oh! would I were a mermaid now,
   For then I'd follow him;
But oh! I'm not a fish-woman,
   And so I cannot swim.   40

" Alas! I was not born beneath
   The Virgin and the Scales,
So I must curse my cruel stars,
   And walk about in Wales."

Now Ben had sailed to many a place
   That's underneath the world;
But in two years the ship came home,
   And all her sails were furled.

But when he called on Sally Brown,
   To see how she went on,   50
He found she'd got another Ben,
   Whose Christian name was John.

" O Sally Brown, O Sally Brown!
   How could you serve me so?
I've met with many a breeze before,
   But never such a blow."

Then reading on his 'bacco box,
   He heaved a bitter sigh,
And then began to eye his pipe,
   And then to pipe his eye.   60

And then he tried to sing " All's Well,"
   But could not though he tried:
His head was turned, and so he chewed
   His pigtail till he died.

His death, which happened in his berth,
   At forty-odd befell:
They went and told the sexton, and
   The sexton toll'd the bell.

                  THOMAS HOOD.

XL. THAT HEATHEN CHINEE

TABLE MOUNTAIN, 1870

These humorous verses come to us from California, where there are a great many Chinese emigrants. The Americans on the Pacific slope are not remarkable for any particular dullness or want of smartness, but occasionally the Oriental is more than a match for them. His ancient tricks are a novelty to the New World.

Euchre, the favourite American gambling game of cards here mentioned, is a variation of the old French game *écarté*.

The Bill Nye spoken of is a slanting allusion to James Nye, a United States official of eminence, whose private taste for card pastimes is well known in his own country. (*Author's Note.*)

WHICH I wish to remark—
    And my language is plain—
That for ways which are dark
    And for tricks that are vain,
The heathen Chinee is peculiar,
    Which the same I would rise to explain.

Ah Sin was his name;
    And I shall not deny
In regard to the same
What that name might imply,   10
But his smile it was pensive and childlike,
    As I frequent remarked to Bill Nye.

It was August the third;
    And quite soft was the skies;

Which it might be inferred
   That Ah Sin was likewise;
Yet he played it that day upon William
   And me in a way I despise.

Which we had a small game,
   And Ah Sin took a hand: 20
It was euchre. The same
   He did not understand;
But he smiled as he sat by the table;
   With the smile that was childlike and bland.

Yet the cards they were stocked
   In a way that I grieve,
And my feelings were shocked
   At the state of Nye's sleeve;
Which was stuffed full of aces and bowers,
   And the same with intent to deceive.   30

But the hands that were played
   By that heathen Chinee,
And the points that he made
   Were quite frightful to see—
Till at last he put down a right bower,
   Which the same Nye had dealt unto me.

Then I looked up at Nye,
   And he gazed upon me;
And he rose with a sigh
   And said, " Can this be?   40
We are ruined by Chinese cheap labour "—
   And he went for that heathen Chinee.

In the scene that ensued
  I did not take a hand,
But the floor it was strewed
  Like the leaves on the strand
With the cards that Ah Sin had been hiding,
  In the game " he did not understand."

In his sleeves, which were long,
  He had twenty-four jacks—   50
Which was coming it strong,
  Yet I state but the facts;
And we found on his nails, which were taper,
  What is frequent in tapers—that's wax.

Which is why I remark,
  And my language is plain,
That for ways that are dark,
  And for tricks that are vain,
The heathen Chinee is peculiar—
  Which the same I am free to maintain.   60

BRET HARTE.

FURTHER NOTES, INCLUDING BIOGRAPHIES

I. SIR PATRICK SPENS. Date, author and occasion of this fine old ballad are quite unknown; but there was much intercourse between Scotland and Norway in old times, and the incident described may be historical.

II. LORD ULLIN'S DAUGHTER. Lines 27 and 28 have been described as "the central jewel" of this fine ballad.

III. HOHENLINDEN. Moreau beat the Austrians at Hohenlinden six months after Campbell had left Bavaria, but he had seen a battle near Ratisbon.

"Subject and spirit, words and music, make an indivisible quaternity, and, except in two or three passages of Homer and Æschylus, there is nothing anywhere that surpasses the last and culminating stanza in poignant simplicity."—PROFESSOR SAINTS-BURY.

32. Old forms of "sepulchre" are "sepulchree" and "sepulchrie."

THOMAS CAMPBELL (1777–1844) was the son of a Glasgow trader. He won high distinction both at the local Grammar School and University, turned to private tuition for support, and won fame at twenty-two with a long poem, *The Pleasures of Hope*. After nearly a year's residence in Germany, and literary hack-work in Scotland, he moved to London and married. *Gertrude of Wyoming* with shorter poems—including *Lord Ullin's Daughter*—was published in 1809. Literary work of all sorts, editorship of the *New Monthly Magazine* for ten years, lectures on poetry, money troubles, ill-health, occasional trips to the continent—such is the record of his remaining years. But in 1825 by a letter to *The Times* he originated the scheme which led to the establishment of London University, " the only important event," he said, " in my life's little history." His last few months were spent in failing health at Boulogne. He was buried in Westminster Abbey, with a guard of Polish nobles, one of whom sprinkled on the coffin a handful of earth from the grave of Kosciusko. His longer poems are now little read, but such things as *Hohenlinden* and the two naval odes are among the chief treasures of English poetry. His *Specimens of the British Poets* is a valuable collection with some interesting criticism.

IV. ROSABELLE. From *The Lay of the Last Minstrel*, canto vi.

13. The gift of second sight, or mental vision, was believed to be widely prevalent in Scotland.

39. Roslin Chapel is famous for its delicate stone-carving, especially the " Prentice Pillar."

V. ALICE BRAND. From *The Lady of the Lake*, canto iv.

46. The fairies wore green, and were offended when mortals wore it.

VI. LOCHINVAR. From *Marmion*, canto v.

43. Cf. *Archie of Cawfield*:

> O, there was horsing, horsing in haste,
> And cracking of whips out owre the lea;

and Byron's " there was mounting in hot haste." This idiom presents an action without specifying the actors.

SIR WALTER SCOTT (1771–1832) was the son of an Edinburgh lawyer. From very early years Scottish legends and Scottish scenery were his delight. At school in Edinburgh his merry pugnacity made him many friends, his omnivorous reading and extraordinary memory stored his mind—and so it was all through his life. Neither at school nor at Edinburgh University, which he entered at twelve, did scholastic subjects make much impression on him, but he was versed in four modern languages and learnt some law in his father's office. Called to the Bar in 1792, he soon published translations from the German, collected and annotated three volumes of *Border Minstrelsy* (which supplied much material for his later original works), and leaped to fame with *The Lay of the Last Minstrel* in 1805. He triumphed again with *Marmion* (1808) and *The Lady of the Lake* (1810), but later poems suffered from their own inferiority and the rising genius of Byron. The canny poet turned to prose, and in 1814 appeared anonymously *Waverley*, the first of the famous series which ended in 1831. Meanwhile Scott had begun to realise his great ambition—to be a landed proprietor. He had married at the age of twenty-six. Now his fame, his wealth, his estate and his hospitality grew and flourished. He was made a baronet in 1820. Six years later came the crash. The publishing house in which he was secretly a partner failed for £117,000; but Scott refused the protection of bankruptcy, worked harder than ever, paid off £40,000 in four years, and soon after his death the remaining debt was paid off by his executors. The effort killed him. Paralysis and other illnesses wore him down. He was taken to Naples in a warship, but hurried home to die at Abbotsford. He was buried in the beautiful ruins of Dryburgh Abbey.

VII. THE HIGH TIDE ON THE COAST OF LINCOLN-SHIRE. " For earnestness and technical excellence one of the finest of modern ballads."—*Dictionary of National Biography*.

101. The tidal wave on the Trent is still called the eygre. Other forms of the word are eagre, higre.

JEAN INGELOW (1820–97) was born at Boston, Lincolnshire, the daughter of a banker. Her first volume of verse appeared in 1850. Tennyson had seen it in manuscript, found some very charming things in it, and advised publication, though he naturally discouraged the practice of rhyming " Eudora " with " before her," and " vista " with " sister." Edward

FitzGerald, the translator of *Omar Khayyám*, liked it so much that he wrote a review, but failed to get it published; and the public failed to read the poems. But in 1863 appeared a volume which went through four editions in a year, and other volumes followed in 1876 and 1885. From 1863 onwards Miss Ingelow lived in London, and wrote a great deal of prose. Her best long novel is said to be *Off the Skelligs* (1872), but her *Stories told to a Child* (1865) are more highly praised.

VIII. HERVÉ RIEL. Published (1871) in the *Cornhill Magazine*; the proceeds (one hundred guineas) were sent by Browning to the distressed people of Paris after the siege. It was composed at Croisic, a little Breton coast town, near the mouth of the Loire. The story is true, but it had been locally quite forgotten.

1. Russell with ninety ships beat Tourville's fifty after a five hours' fight, and thus crushed the French attempt to restore James II.

92. The fourteenth-century *Tour Solidor* still overlooks the south-west harbour of St. Servan.

120. A run of over three hundred miles! Browning has sentimentalised the facts, and ignored geography. Riel really asked to be discharged from the service.

IX. HOW THEY BROUGHT THE GOOD NEWS FROM GHENT TO AIX. Written on board ship, in the reaction after a severe tossing on the Bay of Biscay. No real incident is described, and we must not criticise too closely all the details. The lines certainly stir the blood.

ROBERT BROWNING (1812–89) was born at Camberwell, his father, a man of wide and exact knowledge in literature, being a clerk in the Bank of England. A private school, his father's library, the Dulwich picture gallery, with some riding, fencing and boxing, provided for his ever restless activity. In 1833 appeared *Pauline*, followed by *Paracelsus* (1834) and *Sordello* (1840), long and difficult poems, full of thought and learning. Trips to Russia and Italy preluded many wanderings, and plays and poems poured from his pen. In 1845 came the romance of his life. He made the acquaintance of the invalid poet Elizabeth Barrett, infused into her some of his abounding vitality, rescued her from an autocratic father, and gave her fifteen years of perfect married happiness. He took great risks and he was justified. Nearly all those years were spent in Italy, and the production of poems continued. The rest of his life was spent in London, with holidays in France and Italy. His work may be said to have culminated in *The Ring and the Book* (1868–69), that " great epic of the enormous importance of small things," but it continued to the end of his long life without a sign of diminution of mental vigour. By slow degrees the public became aware of the great worth of his poetry. The famous Browning Society was founded in 1881. Browning himself was much lionised, and he lived a great deal in what is called Society. He knew its value very well, but he was less of a cynic than most men of his powers. He was buried in Westminster Abbey, the choir singing his wife's poem, " He giveth His beloved sleep."

XI. THE BALLAD OF AGINCOURT:

6. Havre was not founded till a hundred years later, by Louis XII. Among the " forts " taken was Harfleur.

39. Referring to line 19.

68. Henry set an ambush in a low-lying meadow.

105 *ff*. Notice how well Drayton works in the proper names, as Scott did later. Shakespeare was often quite careless about this nicety; Prof. Elton quotes the appalling line—" Sir Richard Ketley, Davy Gam, esquire."

MICHAEL DRAYTON (1563–1631) was born near Atherstone in Warwickshire. He seems to have been taken up quite young by a local magnate, Sir Henry Goodere, and well educated for those times; but it is uncertain whether he went to a university. By 1591 he was in London, and fourteen years after Spenser had popularised the pastoral form, Drayton brought out *Idea, The Shepherd's Garland*. Next came the inevitable series of sonnets, but the magnificent " Since there's no help, come, let us kiss and part " was not added till 1619. In 1597 appeared his most popular work, *England's Heroical Epistles*, a series of verse letters between great ill-fated personages, after the manner of Ovid. *The Barons' Wars* of 1603 is a complete remodelling of the earlier *Mortimeriados*. In 1606 came *Odes*, including the first form of *Agincourt*. The next thirteen years were spent on the enormous verse record of the localities and legends of England, called *Poly-Olbion*. Drayton had got into disgrace with James I. by rushing in with a poetic congratulation before he had decently deplored the loss of Elizabeth—who had indeed done nothing for him. However, Prince Henry and Prince Charles accepted in succession the dedication of *Poly-Olbion*, but they could not induce the public to read it. It has, indeed, weary stretches, but contains many passages of much charm. Among Drayton's later work is the charming fairy poem *Nymphidia*. He was buried in Westminster Abbey. He is not known to have married.

XII. THE BATTLE OF NASEBY:

Charles I., "the Man of Blood," led the main body at Naseby, Sir Marmaduke Langdale the cavalry of the left wing, Prince Rupert that of the right; Sir Jacob Astley was one of the commanders of the reserves. Fairfax and Skippon led the main body of the Parliamentary army; Ireton opposed Rupert, and Cromwell Langdale. Rupert broke Ireton's wing, and fighting in the centre was for long indecisive, but Cromwell's complete success on the right secured a crushing victory for Parliament. The supposed author was one of the foot who rallied round their guns after Rupert's rush had passed.

A poet of so utterly different a genius and lot in life as Francis Thompson wrote: " I am disposed to put in a good word for Macaulay's Ballads." Here is a stanza from his own *The Veteran of Heaven*:

O Captain of the wars, whence won Ye so great scars?
　In what fight did Ye smite, and what manner was the foe?
Was it on a day of rout they compassed Thee about,
　Or gat Ye these adornings when Ye wrought their overthrow?

1. In the first stanza the victorious troops are greeted on their return to London.

14. Sir Thomas Fairfax.

22. Alsatia was the Whitefriars sanctuary used by debtors and law-breakers; see Scott's *The Fortunes of Nigel*. The Stewarts' court was at Whitehall.

35. The famous Ironsides, organised by Cromwell to balance the Royalist superiority in cavalry.

37–40. Typical Roundhead calumnies.

55. Oxford was a great centre of royalism.

THOMAS BABINGTON, LORD MACAULAY (1800–59), was born on St. Crispin's Day in Leicestershire. His father, Zachary, a very remarkable man, had been first Governor of the negro colony at Sierra Leone. Macaulay read incessantly from the age of three; before he was eight he had written a compendium of Universal History, and several long poems, perfect in spelling, grammar and punctuation. A private school near his home at Clapham, and another near Cambridge, led to his entering Trinity College in 1818, where he won a fellowship; he was called to the Bar in 1826. Fame arrived with his article on Milton in the *Edinburgh Review* (1825). He entered Parliament in 1830, and soon made a great reputation. In 1833 he went as Member of Council to India, where he set up the Europeanised system of education, and framed the Criminal Code which was enacted after the Mutiny. From 1839 to 1841 he was Secretary for War. The popular *Lays of Ancient Rome* came out in 1842, the brilliant *Essays* continued, and the *History of England*

G

was begun. He lost his seat at Edinburgh in 1847, and settled down to literary work. The *History* had an extraordinary success; it has been translated into at least eleven languages. Honours both foreign and domestic poured upon him. In 1857 he was made a Peer; " God knows," he wrote, " that the poor women at Delhi and Cawnpore are more in my thoughts than my coronet." His positiveness and omniscience have become a by-word. " I wish I was as sure of anything as Tom Macaulay is of everything," said one. The deeper side of his nature must be gathered from Sir George Trevelyan's admirable life of his uncle. He was buried in Westminster Abbey. He never married.

XIII. HAWKE:

1. This " wonderful year " of the Seven Years' War saw also the victory of Minden, and the capture of Quebec by Wolfe.

SIR HENRY JOHN NEWBOLT (1862) was educated at Clifton College, and Corpus Christi College, Oxford: he practised at the Bar (1887–99), and was editor of the *Monthly Review* (1900–4); Vice-president of the Royal Society of Literature; Professor of Poetry and Member of Academic Committee. Some of his works are: *Admirals All* (1897), *Songs of the Sea* and *Songs of the Fleet* (1904–10), *Poems New and Old* (1912), *Tales of the Great War* (1916), *A New Study of English Poetry* (1917), *Submarining and Anti-Submarining* (1918).

ROBERT SOUTHEY (1774–1843) was the son of a Bristol linendraper. Local schools did little for the shy boy, but he read the English poets greedily—later in life he admitted having read *The Faerie Queene* thirty times—and was already an epic poet at twelve. After four years at Westminster School he wrote an article against flogging, in an informal school magazine, proved, in fact, from the ancients and the Fathers, that it was an invention of the Devil. For this crime he had to leave. At eighteen he went up to Balliol College, where again he made few but firm friends. A wonderful scheme for a joint colony on the Susquehanna with Coleridge and other young friends—Pantisocracy they called it—came to nothing. Marriage at twenty-one, the publication of his first epic *Joan of Arc* in the next year, wanderings in England and Portugal, and the continual collection of folios, led to his settling down in 1803 at Greta Hall, Keswick, in joint occupation with his brother-in-law Coleridge. There he supported a growing family by his unwearied pen, writing articles for the *Quarterly Review*, writing poems chiefly epic, histories and lives in prose, almost living in a library which grew to 14,000 volumes. *Thalaba the Destroyer* (1800), *Madoc* (1805), *The Curse of Kehama* (1809), and *Roderick, the Last of the Goths* (1814), are now little read, but the Letters, and the Lives at least of Nelson and Wesley, are still delightful. Overwork and bereavement made his old age sad. He became Poet Laureate in 1813. By his own desire he was buried in Crosthwaite Churchyard.

XV. THE BURIAL OF SIR JOHN MOORE. After his famous retreat through northern Spain before the greatly superior forces of Soult and Ney, Moore was compelled to fight at Corunna in 1809, as the ships sent to take off his army had been delayed. He won the battle but fell himself.

CHARLES WOLFE (1791 – 1843) was educated in England and at Trinity College, Dublin. He took Orders in 1817, and died of consumption at the Cove of Cork, as Queenstown was then called. He is one of the small band of poets who are known for one poem of supreme excellence. It appeared in a Newry paper in 1817, and was ascribed to Byron—who admired it greatly—and to others.

XVI. ADMIRAL HOSIER'S GHOST appeared with great success after Admiral Vernon's capture of Porto Bello in 1739. Two years later Glover's friend Pitt used the popular indignation which the ballad had aroused, in an attack on Walpole's administration. Hannah More heard Glover sing it in advanced old age.

1. Porto Bello on the Caribbean Sea, near the entrance of the present Panama Canal, had in 1597 succeeded Nombre de Dios as the Spanish port for the Peruvian trade, and was often attacked by the English. In 1726 Hosier was sent out with a strong blockading squadron, but 4000 of his men, sixty officers, himself and his two successors, were carried off by fever.

13. Cf. Tennyson's "his heavy-shotted hammock-shroud."

22. The *Burford* was Vernon's ship.

53. Bastimentos, now called Provision Island, was not far from Porto Bello, and served as an anchorage.

RICHARD GLOVER (1712–85) was educated at Cheam school, and followed his father's calling as Hamburg merchant. As Member of Parliament he was frequently the spokesman of the important commercial interest, and was intimate with Pitt, Lyttleton, Temple and Cobham. At sixteen he had written a *Poem to the Memory of Sir Isaac Newton*, and in 1737 appeared *Leonidas*, a blank verse epic in nine books, later enlarged to twelve. " At the time of publication a zeal, or rather rage, for liberty prevailed in England," and the now unreadable epic passed through three editions in two years. A tragedy, *Boadicea*, ran for nine nights at Drury Lane in 1753, and the *Athenaid*, in thirty books, was " presented to the world " after his death; but the world ignored the gift. Glover was evidently a trustworthy man. He was one of two commissioned by the Duchess of Marlborough in her will to write the Life of her great husband; but as the work was to be revised by Lord Chesterfield, whose political character Glover despised, he refused the honour.

ALFRED, LORD TENNYSON (1809–92) was the son of a Lincolnshire clergyman, the fourth of twelve children. At twelve he produced an epic of 6000 lines, and at fourteen a blank verse drama. He had his early education nominally at Louth Grammar School—" How I did hate that school! " was his later testimony— really from his father and his father's library. In 1828 he went up to Trinity College, Cambridge, and next year was successful with his prize poem *Timbuctoo*; but his first characteristic verse was in the volume published in 1830. Two years later appeared *The Lady of Shalott*, *Œnone*, *The Lotos-Eaters*, with other masterpieces, and in 1842 his fame was finally established by two volumes including *Morte d'Arthur* and *Ulysses*. His friend Arthur Hallam had died in 1833, and for many years Tennyson was composing the sections of a great memorial poem, published in 1850 as *In Memoriam*. In the same year he married after an engagement of fourteen years, and succeeded Wordsworth as Poet Laureate—truly a memorable date. In 1853 Tennyson settled down at Farringford, Isle of Wight. *Maud* was produced in 1855, and the first *Idylls of the King* in 1859. Well versed from his youth in Latin and Greek literature, he began Hebrew at the age of fifty-eight, and thought of translating the Book of Job. Having done with the *Idylls* he wrote several plays, of which *Becket* was far the most successful on the stage. Other poems, some of them splendid, continued to appear, and in his eighty-first year he wrote the " immortal lyric " *Crossing the Bar*. He was buried in Westminster Abbey, next his friend Robert Browning.

XIX. The Forsaken Merman. See an eloquent eulogy in Swinburne's *Essays and Studies*, p. 158. Notice how the same rhyme-sounds tend to recur. The music of this beautiful poem is inseparable from its pathetic effect; line 82 hits a blow upon the ear; contrast line 34, and others.

Matthew Arnold (1822–88) was the eldest son of Thomas Arnold, the famous headmaster of Rugby.

His Rugby prize poem, *Alaric at Rome*, was published in 1840. A scholarship at Balliol College, the Newdigate Prize for his poem *Cromwell*, and a fellowship at Oriel, were his chief university successes. He was private secretary to Lord Lansdowne from 1847 to 1851, and in the latter year he married and became an Inspector of Schools. All his life he worked hard and successfully in the cause of better education; his Reports are said to be readable more than most blue-books. Meanwhile a volume of poems had appeared in 1848, and was followed by others. He was Professor of Poetry at Oxford from 1857 to 1867, and several volumes of admirable literary essays embody his professorial work. Twice he lectured in the United States. After his professorship he dropped poetry, and wrote works of social, moral, and religious criticism, *Culture and Anarchy*, *Literature and Dogma*, and others. Much of his criticism, and more of the apt phrases in which he expressed it, have become common property, and at least one pathetic poem, *Sohrab and Rustum*, is known to everyone; but many of his poems are of high excellence. His criticism is criticism of the only useful kind—that which provokes thought, and it is remarkably readable. He was buried in Laleham churchyard, by that Thames which he had loved and praised so well.

XX. JASON'S PLOUGHING:

18. Notice that Morris, like his master Chaucer and all but the most modern writers, uses the Roman names of Greek divinities.

40. Morris places Phineus' town, Salmydessa, on the Propontis or Sea of Marmora.

101. Juno, in the guise of an old woman, had carried Jason over the swollen river Anaurus.

140. The allusion is to the Golden Fleece.

144. The Euripus, which separated Eubœa from the mainland of Greece.

WILLIAM MORRIS (1834–96) was the son of a London broker. He was an early reader, and at four knew most of Scott's novels. Four years at a private school were followed by three at Marlborough College, and in 1853 he went up to Exeter College, Oxford. There he made friends with Edward Burne-Jones, relinquished—with him—his notion of taking Orders, and studied art with characteristic energy. He entered an architect's office in 1856, produced the beautiful *Defence of Guinevere* in 1858, and married in the following year. The building and furnishing of his own house gave him an opportunity of realising that ideal of beauty in every-day things, of which he became the apostle. It was an age of ugliness in England. With Burne-Jones, Rossetti, and a few others, he formed a company to work in metal, to make wallpapers, chintzes, carpets, and stained glass, and his immense enthusiasm was a great element in its success. In 1883 he threw himself heart and soul into the cause of socialism, but not finding human beings as tractable as colours and fabrics, he gradually returned to art and literature. *The Life and Death of Jason* had appeared in 1867, *The Earthly Paradise* was completed in 1870, and the result of two journeys to

Iceland was the long and vigorous *Sigurd the Volsung* of 1876. He translated the *Æneid* and the *Odyssey*, and wrote a number of prose romances. His last six years were mainly devoted to making beautiful things of books; the magnificent *Kelmscott Chaucer* was completed just before his death. " He was buried in Kelmscott churchyard, followed to the grave by the workmen he had inspired, the members of the league which he had supported, the students of the art guild he had founded, and the villagers who had learnt to love him."

XXI. THE HEALING OF CONALL CARNACH. The best parts of the old Irish heroic tradition centre round Connor, King of Ulster (first century A.D.), and his antagonist Maev, Queen of Connaught. Keth was Maev's nephew, Conall Carnach (Conall the Victorious) one of the mightiest and most chivalrous of the Ulster champions.

1. Sliabh Fuad was the highest mountain of the Fews range in County Armagh.

18. The ruins of Maev's palace are still pointed out at Rathcroghan, County Roscommon.

29. Breiffny was a border district between Ulster and Connaught, called after a famous female warrior.

31. On Moy Slaught (the Plain of Adoration) stood the great gold-covered image of Crom Cruach; see line 45. Later he was cursed by St. Patrick, and swallowed in the earth up to his neck.

77. Forbaid, son of Connor, killed Maev, because Keth had similarly smitten Connor.

SIR SAMUEL FERGUSON (1810–86) was born in Belfast, educated there and at Trinity College, Dublin, and called to the Irish bar in 1838. In his twenty-first year he wrote the well-known *Forging of the Anchor*, and almost to the end of his life he wrote prose articles in the reviews and magazines. But his best work was done in the wide and little-cultivated field of Irish antiquities, including Irish sagas. He spent a year on the Continent following the traces of early Irish missionaries and scholars, and his marriage in 1848 gave him an enthusiastic helper in his work. *Lays of the Western Gael* appeared in 1864, and three years later he became the first Deputy Keeper of the Records of Ireland. He was knighted in 1878, and received many honours from learned bodies. Of several masterly poems founded on Irish bardic tales, the long blank-verse *Conary*, published in 1880, is the finest. The art with which the incoherent details of the old story are knit together into a compact and moving poem is not short of consummate. Perhaps his only weakness is a tendency to " tag " the old pagan legends with some reference to the coming Christianity.

XXII. THE DEATH OF CUCHULAIN. Cuchulain, the Achilles of Irish legend, had left Emer and taken a young wife at Emania. Emer's vengeance is here related. The names and details vary greatly in the different legends.

37. Connor's palace had three buildings: " that of the Red Branch, where were kept the heads and arms of vanquished enemies; that of the Royal Branch,

where the kings lodged; and that of the Speckled House, where were laid up the arms of the Ulster warriors."

88. A classical author mentions the combats of the Celts with the sea-waves. There is naturally much sea-magic in the old tales.

WILLIAM BUTLER YEATS (1865) was educated at Godolphin School, Hammersmith, and Erasmus Smith School, Dublin. Some of his works are *The Wanderings of Oisin* (1889), *The Countess Kathleen* (1892), *The Works of William Blake* (joint editor, 1893), *Poems* (1895), *Cathleen ni Hoolihan* (1902), *Ideas of Good and Evil* (1903), *Collected Works* (8 vols. 1908), *Plays for an Irish Theatre* (1912), *Reveries* (1916), *Per Amica Silentia Lunæ* (1918).

XXIII. LA BELLE DAME SANS MERCI. "It would be impertinence to praise this poem, which charms alike young and old; and it stands above the reach of criticism."—THE POET LAUREATE.

JOHN KEATS (1795–1821) was born in Finsbury, where his father kept a livery stable. He worked hard at school in Enfield, and was noted for his generosity and pugnacity; there he learnt Latin, and stored his mind with Greek mythology. It was the *Faerie Queene* that awakened his genius; "he ramped through the scenes of the romance," writes the friend who introduced him, "like a young horse turned into a spring meadow." At fifteen he was apprenticed to a local surgeon, and four years later became a medical student at St. Thomas's and Guy's Hospitals. Friendship with Leigh Hunt and Haydon the painter nourished his imaginative vein. The little volume published in 1817 contains the noble sonnet *On first Looking into Chapman's Homer*, but nothing else of the first rank. In the same year he left London, and worked upon *Endymion* at Carisbrooke, Margate, Canterbury, Oxford, Burford Bridge. This beautiful but immature poem appeared in 1818. The hardships of a real tramp in Scotland deranged his health, and in 1820 he had certain warning of consumption. In the same year were published his best poems, *Lamia, Isabella, The Eve of St. Agnes, Hyperion* and the great *Odes*. Increasing illness, and a late ardent and now hopeless love affair drove him to seek health in Italy. He died and was buried at Rome. No man ever had better or warmer friends. His letters, while health remained, are captivating; *La Belle Dame Sans Merci* comes from a long journal-letter to his brother and sister-in-law in America. He nursed with devotion another brother who died of consumption. The tale of his having been killed by a hostile review is ridiculous.

XXIV. LOVE. "Remarkable for a certain strange fascination of melody . . . noteworthy also as perhaps the fullest expression of the almost womanly softness of Coleridge's character."—H. D. TRAILL.

SAMUEL TAYLOR COLERIDGE (1772–1834) was the youngest of thirteen children of the Vicar of Ottery St. Mary, in Devonshire. He early wrote poetry, though at Christ's Hospital (1782–91) his passion for poetry was temporarily eclipsed by a passion for metaphysics. After three years at Jesus College, Cambridge—in the course of which he put in four months' very inefficient service as a private in the 15th Light Dragoons—he left without taking a degree, met Southey at Oxford, and formed with him a wonderful plan for marrying two Bristol sisters, and emigrating to form an ideal community in America. The marriages, being the cheaper part of the design, duly came off. Lectures at Bristol, a volume of verse (1797), and love in a cottage, then followed. Under the influence of Wordsworth, *The Ancient Mariner* and all his finest poems were composed in the next two years. Then came a visit to Germany with Wordsworth, writing for the *Morning Post*, and settlement at Keswick in 1800. The next phase of his life makes dismal reading—wanderings, vast projects, opium-eating, occasional estrangement from such firm friends as the Wordsworths and Lamb, his family left to Southey's loyal care. In 1816 he put himself under the care of a Highgate doctor, lived in his house for the rest of his life, and recovered some part of his great powers. His lectures on Shakespeare mark an epoch in criticism, and his wonderful gift of talk never left him. There is a pretty picture of Coleridge talking for two hours, while Wordsworth listened with profound attention, now and then nodding his head, though he confessed afterwards that he had understood not one syllable. His best poems are unique in loveliness. Coleridge was buried at Highgate.

XXV. THE SENSITIVE PLANT. "The sensitive plant is of course Shelley himself, 'companionless,' as he makes himself in *Adonais* [the noble elegy on Keats], 'desiring what it has not, the beautiful.'"—STOPFORD BROOKE.

XXVI. ARETHUSA. Alpheus, a river-god of the (Dorian) Peloponnesus, pursued the water-nymph Arethusa under the sea to Sicily, where she became the spring of Ortygia. Shelley treats the old story quite freely. The notion of reconciliation may have come from Virgil's tenth *Eclogue*, line 4, but the treatment is original. After filling our ears with the music of this poem, we might well examine the truth of its details; notice especially lines 10, 18, and 63. Weave, woven, woof, are favourite words with Shelley, partly no doubt for their beautiful sound; but there is a notion of growth, almost of life, in the act of weaving, which suits his animated view of nature.

PERCY BYSSHE SHELLEY (1792–1822) "was born in the purple of the English squirearchy"; but his sympathies were stedfastly revolutionary. We hear first of long country rambles with his sisters, and equally long tales made up for their delight. Two years at a private school led on to Eton in 1804—not a promising nurse for a determined rebel; however his prodigious memory helped him to acquire a certain fluency in Greek and Latin. He published some *very* juvenile prose romances, and entered University College, Oxford, in 1810. There he read with intense eagerness, often sixteen hours a day, but not the official Aristotle. A pamphlet on *The Necessity of Atheism* led to his expulsion, and a breach with his father, Sir Timothy. His marriage at nineteen confirmed that breach, and ended unhappily. His first fine poem *Alastor* appeared in 1816. In that year he married Mary Godwin, and lived in Italy. There he renewed his friendship with Byron, whom he had already met at Geneva, and gave his life to the study of most things and the practice of poetry. In one year he wrote the masterpieces *Prometheus Unbound* and *The Cenci*, besides shorter poems. In his later works the enthusiasm for humanity which first animated him subsides into a more plaintive and personal vein. Always a lover of boats, Shelley with some English friends had a sailing-boat built, fast but cranky, which upset in a squall and went down with the owners. Shelley's body was washed ashore, and cremated by his friends, of whom Byron was one; the ashes were buried at Rome. " A man who has made more sacrifices of his fortune and feelings for others than any I ever heard of "—such was Byron's verdict; and all his friends loved him.

XXVII. Lucy Gray. Solitude had a fascination for Wordsworth; he felt deeply what he calls its "self-sufficing power." This beautiful poem, of which Wordsworth's latest biographer has said that it " will perhaps be remembered when all other English poetry of the century is forgotten," begins and ends on the note of solitude. It is founded on fact; " the way in which the incident is treated," so said the author, "and the spiritualising of the character, might furnish hints for contrasting the imaginative influences which I have endeavoured to throw over common life, with Crabbe's matter-of-fact style of handling subjects of the same kind."

XXVIII. LAODAMIA. This, "the most majestic of his poems, his one great utterance on heroic love," was written fifteen years after *Lucy Gray*. It was inspired by the study of Virgil, and contains many Virgilian echoes. For an adverse criticism see Sara Coleridge's letter to Aubrey de Vere (1846).

79. Hercules rescued Alcestis from Death; Medea by her magic restored Æson to youth. Compare lines 87, 88.

106. Notice the striking contrast with Wordsworth's theory of style, and his own earlier practice.

158. Wordsworth later rejected this merciful conclusion. His stern rectitude seems to have felt it inconsistent with what precedes, especially line 75; Haydon says his wife made him change it. But the best modern opinion prefers the earlier text here given.

WILLIAM WORDSWORTH (1770–1850) was born at Cockermouth, the son of a Cumberland attorney. At nine he went to school at Hawkshead, near Lake Windermere; he read all Fielding, *Don Quixote*, and some of Swift, but chiefly the book of Nature, "his lifelong mistress." In 1787 he went up to St. John's College, Cambridge. He was probably the first undergraduate who ever spent a long vacation (1790) walking

in Switzerland. Having taken his degree, after a short
stay in London he spent more than a year in France,
sympathising, almost co-operating, with the moderate
revolutionaries. When the extremists got their way,
Wordsworth passed through a period of despondency
from the wreck of his high hopes for humanity. From
this he was saved by the companionship of his sister
Dorothy. Intercourse with Coleridge led to the joint
volume of *Lyrical Ballads* in 1798—an epoch in English
poetry. He settled at Grasmere in 1800, married two
years later—Dorothy being still a comrade—and
moved to Rydal Mount in 1813. Tours in Scotland
and on the Continent, occasional visits to London, and
his succession to Southey as Poet Laureate in 1843,
are the chief external events to record. His stubborn
affection was deeply tried by the mental collapse of
Dorothy. Gradually his poetry gained the public ear,
and has ever since been a formative influence and a
consoling power; but nearly all his finest work was
done in the first half of his life; his high and holy
purpose never failed, but his once fervid imagination
cooled, and his ear grew dull to beauty. He was buried
by his own desire in Grasmere churchyard.

XXIX. THE HERMIT. This story is from that medi-
æval storehouse of tales, *Gesta Romanorum*; but it
had been treated by several English writers before
Parnell. It is probably of Oriental origin.

THOMAS PARNELL (1679–1717) was born in Dublin,
his father having gone to Ireland at the Restoration.
At thirteen he entered Trinity College, Dublin, and

was ordained in 1700. He became Archdeacon of
Clogher in 1705, but he was not exactly a model parson,
for " as soon as ever he had collected in his annual
revenues, he immediately set out for England, to enjoy
the company of his dearest friends." He was always
welcome in that brilliant company which included
Pope, Swift, Arbuthnot and Gay; and when Parnell felt
a fit of spleen coming on—he suffered a good deal from
that ambiguous disorder—" he returned with all speed
to the remote parts of Ireland," and wrote dolorous
descriptions of his surroundings. In London the wits
criticised each other's productions, and played tricks
on one another, especially on Swift. Parnell contributed notes and a Life of Homer to Pope's translation
of the *Iliad*; and Pope's letters are most affectionate
in tone; he collected and published the poems after
Parnell's death. Parnell may be said to live by *The
Hermit*, though *A Fairy Tale* is pleasant reading and
not in the least ponderous. He translated *Pervigilium
Veneris* and *Batrachomyomachia*, and wrote enormous
dissertations in verse on the heroes of the Old
Testament. He was buried at Chester, where he died
on his way to Ireland. His wife had died after two
years of married life.

XXX. ALEXANDER'S FEAST. .

25. Alexander encouraged, from policy, the opinion
that Jove was his father.

29. This seems to mean erect like a cork-screw.
Such was the form assumed by Satan in *Paradise
Lost*, ix. 496.

37–40. Dr. Verrall says: "The see-saw is mock majesty, the self-complacency of the drop too much." Young actually chose the metre of these lines for his *Ode on the Ocean*, on account of its majesty!

72. Notice that the "hand" is Timotheus', the "pride" Alexander's.

97. The Lydian mode (or style) in Greek music was soft and voluptuous.

165. A long-drawn note was not possible on the old stringed instruments, which were twanged like a harp, not played with a bow; and even the notes of wind instruments were limited in duration by the capacity of human lungs.

169. Legend says that an angel came down from heaven, to listen to St. Cecilia's playing on her new invention. But the skies to which Timotheus raised Alexander are not precisely those which the angels inhabit. The rhetorical point of the last two lines is excusable only on the ground, as Dr. Verrall says, that Dryden did not take Cecilia seriously.

JOHN DRYDEN (1631–1700) was the eldest of fourteen children; his father was a justice of the peace for Northamptonshire. He was educated at Westminster School, under the famous Dr. Busby, to whom he afterwards confided the care of his two sons. In 1750 he went up to Trinity College, Cambridge, and took his degree in due course. He must have worked hard, but he was not precocious; his first poem of mark, *Heroic Stanzas* in memory of Cromwell, appeared in 1658. On the Restoration, he eulogised Charles II. with equal

fervour; indeed his opinions, both political and literary, were always rather fluid. In 1683 he made an
unhappy marriage with a lady of title. He had been
elected a Fellow of the newly formed Royal Society,
and we soon find him among the wits of Will's Coffee
House, where he presently reigned supreme. His
rhymed plays won success by degrees, and in 1668
appeared his prose *Essay of Dramatic Poesie*. In 1670
he became Poet Laureate. His real admiration for
Milton was oddly shown by turning *Paradise Lost* into
an opera, with the author's permission. But his true
powers were shown in the great satires, *Absalom and
Achitophel* (1681), *The Medal* and *MacFlecknoe* (1682),
and poems of religious controversy—perhaps the only
readable things of the kind—*Religio Laici* (1682) and
The Hind and the Panther (1687); he had turned
Roman Catholic in 1686. He lost the Laureateship at
the Revolution, and took to play-writing again. His
translation of Virgil and *Alexander's Feast* appeared
in 1697, and the *Fables*, which show his genius at its
height, in 1700. He was buried with great state in
Westminster Abbey.

XXXI. On the Death of a Favourite Cat.
Horace Walpole had two cats. Gray did not know
which had been drowned, hence the confusion of
colours in lines 4 and 10.

1. Notice the parody of Dryden's opening to *Alexander's Feast*.

8. The "fair round face" is from Pope's *Wife of
Bath*. Gray's poems are wonderful mosaics, made

from phrases of other writers, and wrought with consummate art into a beautiful whole. If anyone thinks it easy to write a fine poem with other men's phrases, let him try it.

15. The Romans imagined each locality to have its guardian spirit, or *genius loci*.

34. Nereids were the fifty daughters of the sea-god Nereus. They sometimes helped shipwrecked sailors or vessels; and dolphins rescued drowning men in the old stories. See *Faerie Queene* iv. 11, stanza 23.

42. Dr. Johnson justly remarked that the story does not logically convey the last moral drawn from it: "if what glistered had been gold, the cat would not have gone into the water; and if she had, would not less have been drowned." Gray allows himself a piece of mock-logic in this mock-heroic poem.

THOMAS GRAY (1716–71) was born in Cornhill, the son of a merchant. At about eleven he went to Eton, where his friendship with Horace Walpole began, and he became what he remained, a scholar and a moralist; his poetry was for long confined to Latin verses and occasional translations. In 1734 Gray entered Peterhouse, Cambridge. The years 1739–41 were spent abroad with Walpole. He then lived with his mother and aunts at Stoke Pogis, and there in 1742 he wrote his first complete poem, the *Ode to Spring*; also the *Ode on a Distant Prospect of Eton College*, and *On Adversity*, and began the famous *Elegy*, finished in 1750. He spent five years at Cambridge in the study of all Greek literature, taking "verse and prose together, like bread and cheese," years which ended with the famous cat poem, sent in a letter to Walpole in 1747. The *Elegy* was published, almost in spite of the author, in 1751, and had an immediate and lasting success. He now made a new start with the great Pindaric Odes, *The Progress of Poesy* (1754), and *The Bard*, which took two and a half years to compose, and owed its completion to the impulse of a Welsh harper's music. Gray refused the Laureateship in 1757, and accepted the chair of Modern Literature and Modern Languages at Cambridge in 1768; but he never lectured. Tours in Scotland and the English lakes found his early love of the picturesque fully maintained. His last poems are remarkable as a foretaste of the later romantic movement; indeed he was in several ways before his age. He unbends delightfully in his excellent *Letters*. He never married. He was buried at Stoke Pogis, in the churchyard which he has made known all over the world.

XXXII. THE NEEDLESS ALARM. " In its humble way, one of the most perfect of human compositions.— GOLDWIN SMITH.

XXXIII. THE COLUBRIAD. The energy of these compact lines where not a word is wasted, the rigid relevance of all the details, and the colloquial vigour of the vocabulary, contribute to make a quite unique little poem.

De Grasse was a French admiral beaten by Hood and captured in 1782 by Rodney. His long queue tied

up with ribbons was fine material for English carica-
turists, especially Gillray.

WILLIAM COWPER (1731–1800) was born in his
father's rectory at Berkhampstead. At the age of
six he lost his mother, whose tenderness he com-
memorated fifty years later in some beautiful lines.
An unhappy time at a boarding-school, and two years
in the house of " a female oculist of great renown "
—for the good of his eyes—led to Westminster School.
There he became a good classical scholar, and has left
a pleasant account of his master, Vincent Bourne.
After leaving at eighteen, he was articled for three
years to an attorney, lived in the Temple, and dabbled
in journalism. At thirty-two his delicate constitution
broke down, but after about two years in a private
asylum he recovered, and settled at Huntingdon as a
boarder with the Rev. William Unwin, whose widow
became two years later his staunch comrade and house-
keeper at Olney. She tended him with unfailing love
during sixteen months of another mental collapse.
Gardening and the care of three tame hares now
occupied him, and urged by Mrs. Unwin he wrote a
series of Moral Satires. But he was too kindly for a
satirist. Friendship with the vivacious and fashion-
able Lady Austin inspired *John Gilpin, The Loss of
the Royal George* (a wonder of simple majesty), and the
long and fine poem *The Task*. This was published in
1782, and made Cowper famous. The advent of his
cousin Lady Hesketh inspired a number of the admirable short poems. But he over-worked himself with

a blank verse translation of Homer (1784–91). Mrs. Unwin lost her faculties and died in 1796, and though other good friends were found, his last years were passed in gloom. Cowper's *Letters* are some of the best in the language.

XXXV. THE HAUNCH OF VENISON.

10. The phrase " potatoes and point " describes this frugal and imaginative form of relish; it also suggests distressing poverty, and admirable self-control.

21. Sir Joshua Reynolds, the great painter, was another member of the Johnson and Burke fraternity.

XXXVI. ELEGY ON THE DEATH OF A MAD DOG.

28 *ff*. This is an adaptation of a Greek epigram, copied by Voltaire, of a man and a snake.

OLIVER GOLDSMITH (1728–74), the son of an Irish clergyman, was educated at village schools and at Trinity College, Dublin. He took his degree in 1749 and inclined to medicine, which he studied after false starts at various professions. This merely nominal study was continued at Edinburgh and Leyden, and in 1754 his rambling, unpractical character sent him travelling about the Continent on foot, with a flute for his companion. Two years later he was in London. After a miserable experience as usher in a Peckham " academy " he took to writing criticism for the reviews, on the edge of utter destitution. *An Enquiry into the Present State of Polite Learning in Europe* attracted some attention, and in 1760 he contributed to the *Public Ledger* a series of articles published two years later as *The Citizen of the World*. In the following year Johnson saved him from immediate distress by selling the manuscript of *The Vicar of Wakefield* for £60, but it was not published till Goldsmith's fame was established by the appearance of his poem, *The Traveller*, in 1764. Two years later the famous novel appeared, and went through three editions in six months. At intervals of two years were produced the comedy *The Goodnatured Man*, the poem *The Deserted Village*, and the comedy *She Stoops to Conquer*, and in two years more Goldsmith was dead. He never married. His grave in the burial ground of the Temple Church cannot now be identified; but at Reynolds's suggestion a monument was erected in Westminster Abbey with a stately Latin inscription by Johnson, which states that he handled almost every kind of literary composition, and adorned them all. Let us add that he had a great gift of humour, and what always goes with it—a tender heart.

XXXVII. Llyn-y-Dreiddiad-Vrawd. Peacock was no admirer of war. Read his admirable *War Song of Dinas Vawr*.

Thomas Love Peacock (1785–1866) was the son of a London glass merchant. He had his schooling from eight to thirteen at Eaglefield Green, and at sixteen moved to London with his mother. We hear dimly of mercantile occupations, and definitely of arduous linguistic labours at the British Museum, and two volumes of verse. In 1808–9 he was for six months private secretary to Sir Home Popham on board the *Venerable*, which he genially describes as "this floating inferno." In 1810 appeared his first work of note, *The Genius of the Thames*. In 1812 Peacock met Shelley, was his continual companion for some years, and later the recipient of his remarkable letters from abroad. The first of his very original novels, *Headlong Hall*, appeared in 1815, and *Nightmare Abbey*, which contains a lively portrait of Shelley, followed three years later. Successive years now saw his appointment at the India House, and his marriage with Miss Jane Gryffydh, whom he had only met eight years before in Wales, and whose hand he now courageously acquired by post. His rather paradoxical article on *The Four Ages of Poetry* is chiefly notable for having provoked Shelley's *Defence of Poetry*. *Maid Marian* (1822), *The Misfortunes of Elphin* (1829), and *Crotchet Castle* (1831), are delightful specimens of Peacockian comedy. In 1836 he succeeded James Mill as Chief Examiner of Indian Correspondence. It is interesting now to find that he prepared a memorandum on a projected Euphrates expedition; he also secured the construction of iron steamers, till then unknown, for navigation to India. His evidence before Parliamentary Committees is said to reveal very considerable powers of mind—as indeed one would only expect in a friend of Shelley; and he had humour and a pleasant vein of sarcasm, in both of which Shelley was conspicuously deficient.

XXXVIII. THE BATTLE OF LIMERICK. "*The Battle of the Baltic* [Campbell] and *The Battle of the Shannon* [*sic*] are two masterpieces of lyric narrative, the one triumphant in tragedy, the other transcendant in comedy."—SWINBURNE.

This appeared in *Punch*, 13th May, 1848. William Smith O'Brien was a leader of the Young Ireland party, a deputation from which had been received by the French government on 3rd April, and the soirée here celebrated had been held on 29th April. The movement was not entirely humorous. Mitchell, editor of the *United Irishman*, was transported; O'Brien, Meagher and others were condemned to death, but the sentences were reduced to transportation. After eight years an amnesty was granted to O'Brien.

7. A mixture of William III. and his general in Ireland, the Duke of Schomberg.

49, 53. Bohea and congou are kinds of Chinese tea.

96. " To cut one's stick " means " to clear out."

107. Peelers, also called Bobbies, from Sir Robert Peel who invented the policeman.

WILLIAM MAKEPEACE THACKERAY (1811–63) was born at Calcutta, where his father was secretary to the Board of Revenue. He was brought home at six, showed an early taste for drawing, went to private schools, and was at Charterhouse from 1822 to 1828. It seems to have been a rough place in those days; Thackeray showed no promise as a scholar, but made a name by his humorous verses. His two years at Trinity College, Cambridge, served to make some good friends—Edward FitzGerald, Kinglake, Tennyson, and Venables who had broken Thackeray's nose in a fight at school. Some residence at Weimar gave him materials for the later description of court life in Pumpernickel. He read law in London, and tried to get his caricatures published. Then his considerable fortune somehow disappeared, he determined to be an artist, and in 1834 settled in Paris. There he married an Irish lady, and was soon back in London, trying journalism. The *Yellowplush Papers* in *Fraser's Magazine* (1838) is the first work we associate with Thackeray. His wife fell ill, and despite his devoted nursing had to be sent to a home, where she long survived her husband in a state of gentle imbecility. Much of his work, both of pen and pencil, was now done in *Punch*, to which he contributed the *Snob Papers* that first made him famous. His masterpiece, *Vanity Fair*, came out in monthly numbers with his own illustrations (1847–48), and gradually became popular. *Pendennis, Lectures on the English Humorists* (given in England and America), *Esmond, The Newcomes, Lectures on the Four Georges* (given in America, and repeated all over England), followed in succession. Thackeray was the first editor of the *Cornhill Magazine* (1860–62); it was a great success; several of his novels with his illustrations came out in it; and it brought him a welcome £4000 a year. In reading Thackeray we think of Shakespeare's Cassius:

> He is a great observer and he looks
> Quite through the deeds of men;

but Tennyson held him " a lovable man," and he was devoted to children.

THOMAS HOOD (1799–1845) was the son of a London

bookseller. After some private schooling he entered a merchant's counting-house at the age of thirteen, but his health could not stand the confinement. Next he was articled to an engraver, with the same result, and then he took to literature. In 1824 he married a sister of Keats's friend, J. H. Reynolds, and Lamb's pathetic lines *On an Infant Dying as soon as Born* relate to their first child. The long and pleasing *Plea of the Mid-summer Fairies* appeared in 1827, and two years later Hood became editor of *The Gem*, which printed much good verse including the editor's *Dream of Eugene Aram*. Then Hood experienced Scott's collapse without having enjoyed his prosperity. The failure of a publisher ruined him, but he was just as heroic as Scott had been; he refused the protection of the law, and spent five years (1835–40) abroad, writing to clear off his liabilities. Then he was editor of the *New Monthly Magazine* for three years, and produced therein his most characteristic long poem, *Miss Kilman-segg and her Precious Leg*. The famous *Song of a Shirt* appeared anonymously in *Punch* in 1843. His health finally broke down in 1844, and he never again rose from his bed. Hood was equally master of the most grotesque wit and the most refined pathos. Few poems can compare with *The Bridge of Sighs*, and none with *Miss Kilmansegg*. The latter is a perfect debauch of wit, pervaded by a grim earnestness of satire which helps the reader through.

FRANCIS BRET HARTE (1839–92) was born at Albany, New York, the son of a schoolmaster. After the usual schooling he went to California at the age of seventeen, and there played many parts—teacher, miner, printer, express-messenger, secretary of the San Francisco mint, and editor. Such experience supplied him with valuable materials, but his first publication was literary in origin, *Condensed Novels* (reissued in 1870), a series of parodies in miniature on well-known writers, which may still be read with pleasure. His fame rests on a few prose sketches of mining life, especially *The Luck of Roaring Camp* and *The Outcasts of Poker Flat*, and two or three poems. Probably few people have read his forty-four volumes, but his best things are inimitable. The sympathetic insight which made him so good a parodist of literature, enabled him also to divine the thoughts and feelings of those rough, inarticulate characters which he drew so well. He was in succession Professor in the University of California and United States consul at Crefeld and at Glasgow; from 1885 he lived in London doing literary work.